Computer Sc
Laboratory Manual Using C++

BRENDA C. PARKER

JUDITH A. HANKINS

J. MACK THWEATT

MIDDLE TENNESSEE STATE UNIVERSITY

Minneapolis/St. Paul   New York   Los Angeles   San Francisco

WEST'S COMMITMENT TO THE ENVIRONMENT

In 1906, West Publishing Company began recycling materials left over from the production of books. This began a tradition of efficient and responsible use of resources. Today, up to 95% of our legal books and 70% of our college texts and school texts are printed on recycled, acid-free stock. West also recycles nearly 22 million pounds of scrap paper annually—the equivalent of 181,717 trees. Since the 1960s, West has devised ways to capture and recycle waste inks, solvents, oils, and vapors created in the printing process. We also recycle plastics of all kinds, wood, glass, corrugated cardboard, and batteries, and have eliminated the use of Styrofoam book packaging. We at West are proud of the longevity and the scope of our commitment to the environment.

Production, Prepress, Printing and Binding by West Publishing Company.

 TEXT IS PRINTED ON 10% POST CONSUMER RECYCLED PAPER

Table of Contents

Preface

In recent years, computer science educators have supported the "closed lab" concept to aid in educational quality and the understanding of students in this field. Students participating in a closed lab environment have a weekly, scheduled and supervised laboratory assignment which is completed at this time period. It is similar to the laboratory structure that has existed for many years in other scientific areas such as chemistry and physics, for example.

This lab manual is the outgrowth of our experiences with the "closed lab" concept. The laboratory exercises in this lab manual have been tested and revised numerous times over the years and have been accepted well within our department. Each lab is designed to provide students with meaningful learning experiences and to expose them to alternative experiences quite different from the typical lecture environment. This lab manual is a "hands-on" guide to an introduction to problem solving and programming in C++.

A disk is available with this manual. Instructors should contact the West Publishing Company representative to obtain disk copies to be distributed to the students. The disk contains all data files and program files needed for the closed labs. If a main frame or mini-computer system is used by the class, instructors are encouraged to upload these files to the system and require students to copy all files into their individual accounts during Lab 1.

We wish to offer special thanks to Dr. Thomas Cheatham, Middle Tennessee State University (MTSU), and Ms. Angela Jordan, MTSU, in providing us with special help in the creation and editing of this manual. Their many contributions to this manual are very sincerely appreciated.

Features
-numerous actual examples of C++ programs
-tutorial in nature
-reinforcement of topics

Audience
-beginning students in computer science
-anyone interested in learning good algorithm development, problem solving and
 programming

Suggestions
-used in a two hour time period structure
-most topics should be previously introduced in lecture

Environment
-microcomputer lab

-Borland's Turbo C++ compiler

Notes to the student
-read each lab carefully
-don't hesitate to ask questions if you do not understand

Notes to the instructor
-encourage team approach
-provide close supervision
-attempt to introduce major topics in lecture previous to requiring each lab activity

Lab 1

Introduction to Programming

Objectives:	**Learn to use the Turbo C++ programming environment to create, edit, compile, link, save and execute a C++ program**

Note: You will be asked to turn in written work for this lab. Please use the provided answer sheet at the end of this lab to indicate all answers for the exercises.

A. Introduction

In the early days of computing, all computers were programmed using machine language since that is the only language that the computer really "understands". However, today programmers use high level languages (languages very close to the spoken word). Examples of high level languages include C++, C, BASIC, FORTRAN, and Pascal. Today programmers may use C++, for example, to provide instructions to the computer instead of using machine language (object code). Since the only language that a computer understands is machine language, we must have some type of translator which is able to take a C++ program (source code) and translate this code to machine language. This translator is called a **compiler**. A C++ compiler is a program which takes C++ source code and translates this code into object code (the machine language version of the C++ source code). This lab is an introduction to Borland's Turbo C++ compiler and its programming environment.   Goals for this lab include:

  1)   Learn how to type in a C++ program
  2)   Learn how to correct errors in typing
  3)   Learn how to compile a C++ program

1

4) Learn how to save a C++ program permanently
5) Learn how to execute a C++ program
6) Learn how to print a C++ program

B. Integrated Development Environment

Turbo C++ uses Integrated Development Environment (IDE) to perform all of the above operations and numerous others. IDE is a programming environment which utilizes windows and menus to allow the user to make selections. Therefore, to accomplish our goals for this lab we need to first make sure that each of the following terms is understood.

A **window** is a rectangular area on the screen that will display information. A computer screen can be divided up into several windows. One window may display a C++ program while another window may display the output of the C++ program.

A **menu bar** is a list of command options. Pull down menus are menus that appear when one of the menu bar choices is selected. A sample menu bar which is displayed by Turbo C++ is shown below.

```
= File  Edit  Search  Run  Compile  Debug  Project  Options  Window  Help
```

```
F1 Help | Open, arrange, and list windows
```

Figure 1   Opening Menu

Each selection has a pull-down menu associated with it. For example, if we choose the word FILE from the above menu, another menu will appear below the word FILE. We call this second menu a pull down menu because it appears on the screen as if it had been "pulled down" from the word FILE similar to the way a window shade is "pulled down" from the top of a window. The following pull-down menu appears when the word FILE is selected using Turbo C++:

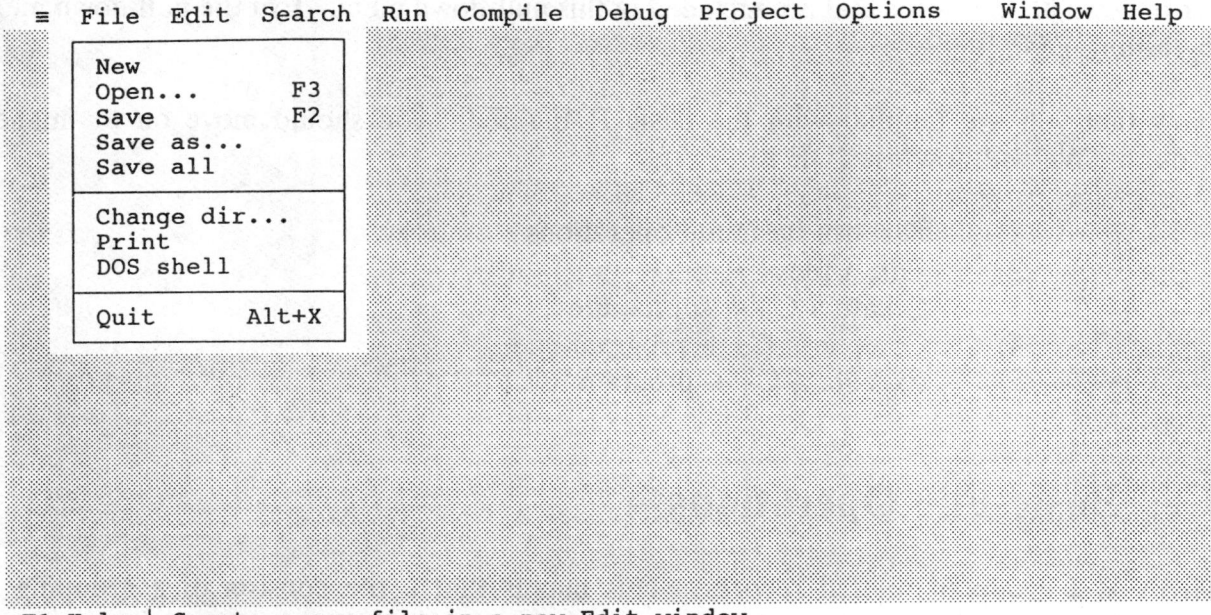

```
≡  File  Edit  Search  Run  Compile  Debug  Project  Options    Window  Help
   ┌──────────────────────┐
   │ New                  │
   │ Open...          F3  │
   │ Save             F2  │
   │ Save as...           │
   │ Save all             │
   │──────────────────────│
   │ Change dir...        │
   │ Print                │
   │ DOS shell            │
   │──────────────────────│
   │ Quit          Alt+X  │
   └──────────────────────┘



 F1 Help │ Create a new file in a new Edit window
```

Figure 2   Pull Down Menu

Let's practice using IDE menus and windows.

EXERCISE 1:   Load TURBO C++ by typing **tc** at the **C** prompt. Write down all the menu selections that appear on the menu bar. **NOTE:** This is the customary way to load the TURBO C++ program. Please check with your instructor if your installation uses a different method to load the C++ compiler.

The menu selections on the menu bar may be "activated" using one of two methods: Mouse activation or function key activation.

EXERCISE 2:   MOUSE ACTIVATION: Locate the mouse cursor on the screen and click on **EDIT**. This means to position the mouse cursor on the menu selection **EDIT** and hit or "click" the left mouse button one time. Now you should be able to see the pull-down menu related to **EDIT**. Write down all words included in the pull-down menu for the **EDIT** menu selection. Exit the pull down menu by hitting the **ESC** key or by clicking the mouse in an area outside the menu.

EXERCISE 3:   Note that there are several prompts at the bottom of the screen which indicate the purpose for several function keys. Write down the purpose of each of the function keys listed at the bottom of the screen.

EXERCISE 4:   FUNCTION KEY ACTIVATION: Hopefully, you noted that there is a function key called **F10** which is used to activate the menu bar. Press the **F10** key and use the arrow keys to select the word **COMPILE** from the menu options. Press **<ENTER>** and write down all the words that are included in this pull-down menu. Exit the pull-down menu by hitting **ESC**.

Now that you are familiar with the basic IDE screen, you should move on to "higher" ground. We will now use IDE to:

1)   Perform basic file operations
2)   Edit a file
3)   Create a C++ source file
4)   Compile a C++ program and
5)   Execute a C++ program

C.   Basic File Operations

A **file** is a group of related records. This means that a file consists of a grouping of instructions and/or data. Examples of files include a listing of commands, a program, or a text document. File operations include activities such as loading a file, saving a file, deleting a file, printing a file, etc. These file activities are easily accomplished by always referring to the unique name given to a file when it is created. If we wish IDE to retrieve a file from a secondary storage device, for example, we must inform IDE of the name of the file and also indicate which disk drive to retrieve the file from. Note the following methods for file manipulations. **Do not perform these operations at this time!**

LOADING A FILE: Press **F3** for **OPEN** and then specify the drive and the name of the file to be opened or loaded to memory.

SAVING A FILE: Press **F2** for **SAVE** and then specify the drive and the name under which the file is to be stored.

PRINTING A FILE: Activate the **FILE** menu selection and then choose **PRINT**.

In the following exercises, we will be performing basic file operations. Before you perform these operations, however, you need to make sure that Turbo C++ always stores information (files) on your own, personal diskette. The default drive should be set to the disk drive which contains your diskette.

EXERCISE 5: Change the default disk drive to the appropriate drive for your class. To accomplish this, activate the menu bar, select the **FILE** menu and the **"Change Dir..."** option. Type

        a: if your diskette is in the **a** drive

        or

        b: if your diskette is in the **b** drive

This will allow Turbo to store files and retrieve all files to/from the disk located in the specified drive.

EXERCISE 6: Load the file called **lab1.txt** to memory from your diskette . Remember that it is not necessary to specify the drive name provided you were able to change the default directory in **Exercise 5**. Therefore, to load the **lab1.txt** file, press **F3** for **OPEN** and then type:

        lab1.txt (if you wish to load the file from the default drive)

        or

        b:lab1.txt (if you wish to load the file from the **b** drive)

        or

        a:lab1.txt (if you wish to load the file from the **a** drive)

D. Editing a File using IDE

To edit a file means to modify or change a file which has been previously created. The IDE editor (processor in IDE which performs editing functions) is a full screen editor. This means that your screen will be used to display part of the file while you work on it. You can think of the screen as a window into your file. What you see on the screen is what will be in your file. All editors display a cursor on the screen denoting where an action will occur when characters are typed. The cursor may be easily moved by using arrow keys on the keyboard. Some common editing functions include: deleting a word or group of words, moving words, searching and replacing words, inserting words or lines, cutting and pasting groups of words.

In **Exercise 6** you loaded a file called **lab1.txt** from your diskette. Let's practice editing this file at this time.

EXERCISE 7: Use the editing features of IDE and make the following changes in this file:

    a)   Correct the spelling of the word "computers" on line 1.

    b)   Correct the spelling of the word "congratulations" in paragraph 2, line 1.

    c)   Change "robots" to "computer controlled robots" in paragraph 1.

    d)   Insert a blank line between paragraph 1 and paragraph 2.

    e)   Delete the line in the document which has been duplicated in paragraph 2.

    f)   Insert your name and date at the beginning of the document.

EXERCISE 8:   Save this newly edited file (press **F2**) and use the same name, **lab1.txt**. Be sure to save this file on **your** disk. To save this file on a disk in drive b, type **b:lab1.txt** when asked for the name of the file. If you type in **lab1.txt**, the file will be saved on the disk in the default drive. Obtain a hardcopy of this file (print the file to the printer). This is accomplished by selecting **FILE** from the menu bar and then selecting the **PRINT** option. **Note**: Your instructor may have additional (or different) instructions to produce this hardcopy on your system.

EXERCISE 9:   Close the file at this time by selecting **WINDOW** from the title bar and then choosing the **CLOSE ALL** option.

E.   Creating, Compiling and Running a C++ program

Now that we have practiced editing a file, we will practice creating a file. To do this we need to inform IDE that we will be working with a new file.

EXERCISE 10:   Choose **FILE** from the menu bar and then choose the word **NEW**. This will allow us to create a new file.

EXERCISE 11:   Type in the following C++ program exactly as it appears below. Type in your name after the word **AUTHOR**.

```
//AUTHOR:
#include <iostream.h>
void main ()
{
        cout<<"Welcome to the world";
        cout<<endl;
        cout<<"     of computing";
        cout<<endl;
        cout<<"          and";
        cout<<endl;
        cout<<"welcome to computer science";
        cout<<endl;
        return;
}
```

EXERCISE 12:   Save this file under the name **example.cpp**. Note that all Turbo C++ files must have the extension "cpp" to indicate that the file is a C++ source file. Also, be sure to indicate the specified drive -- type **b:example.cpp** if you are saving this file on the disk in drive b.

After you have finished typing in your source code (the above program), two additional files must be created: the **.obj** file and the **.exe** file. Let's briefly discuss these two files.

First, a source file must be translated into machine language so that the computer will be able to understand the instructions. In other words, the computer needs to create an object program (.obj) which is the machine language version of the above program. This object program is created by the compiler.

Secondly, all object programs may need various library programs in order to execute. For example, the above program cannot be executed without the <iostream.h> file which contains information about input/output. Thus, various other files may need to be linked or added to the .obj file. We call this newly created file the .exe file. The .exe file, then, is the only file in C++ which can be executed.

The source program must be compiled and linked before the instructions in the program can be executed. There are several methods for compiling and creating the .exe file in IDE:

1) Select the word **COMPILE** from the menu bar.
    The **COMPILE** command compiles the active file and creates an .obj file, if there are no errors.
2) Press **F9 MAKE**.
    The **MAKE** command creates both the .obj and the .exe file but doesn't execute the program.
3) Press **ALT-F9 Compile**.
    ALT-F9 creates an .obj file, if there are no errors.
4) Select **RUN** from the menu bar.
    The **RUN** command creates an .obj file and an .exe file. It also executes the program.

All of the above commands will place the .obj and the .exe files on the diskette in the default drive which is **a** or **b**, depending on which was set as the default in Exercise 5.

EXERCISE 13:   Let's use one of the easier methods for compilation. Hit the **F9 Make** function key at this time.

At this point the compiler will display messages related to the success or failure of the compilation process.

EXERCISE 14:   Study the following sample of a compiler message and indicate all information displayed by the compiler. (Number of errors, number of warnings, etc.)

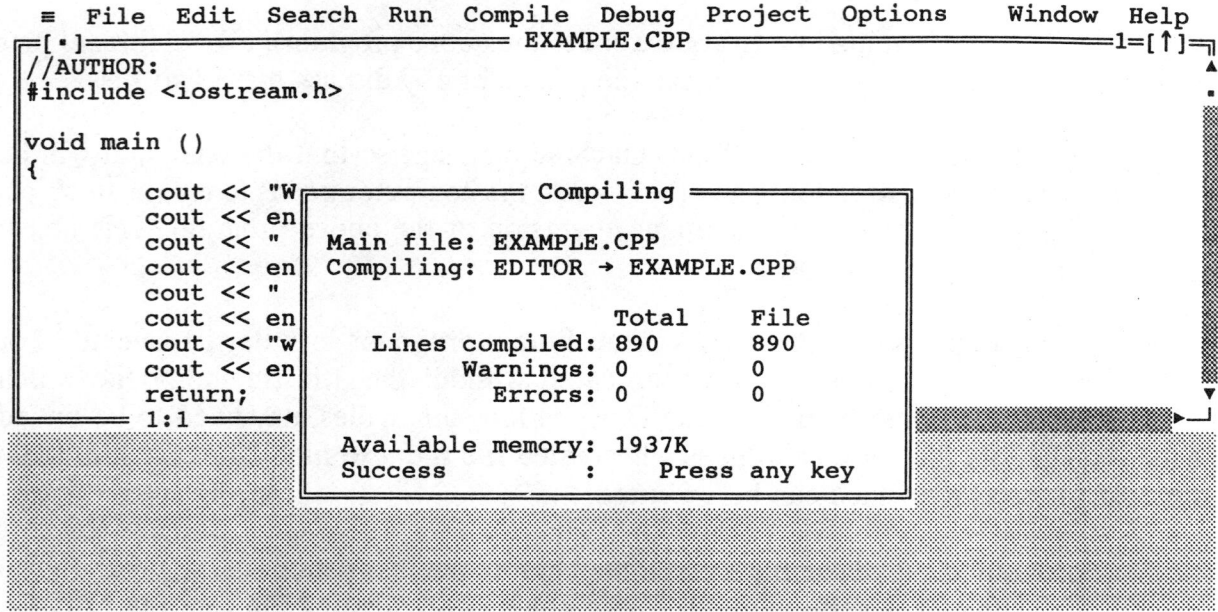

```
 ≡  File  Edit  Search  Run  Compile  Debug  Project  Options    Window  Help
╔═[•]═══════════════════════════ EXAMPLE.CPP ════════════════════════════1=[↑]═╗
║//AUTHOR:                                                                     ▲
║#include <iostream.h>                                                        ·
║
║void main ()
║{
║        cout << "W╔══════════════════ Compiling ═══════════════╗
║        cout << en║                                             ║
║        cout << " ║  Main file: EXAMPLE.CPP                     ║
║        cout << en║  Compiling: EDITOR → EXAMPLE.CPP            ║
║        cout << " ║                                             ║
║        cout << en║                        Total    File        ║
║        cout << "w║    Lines compiled: 890         890          ║
║        cout << en║         Warnings: 0            0            ║
║        return;   ║           Errors: 0            0            ║▼
║═════ 1:1 ══════◄ ║                                             ║►═╝
║                  ║  Available memory: 1937K                    ║
║                  ║  Success          :     Press any key       ║
║                  ╚═════════════════════════════════════════════╝
║
╚════════════════════════════════════════════════════════════════════════════╝
 F1 Help  Alt-F8 Next Msg  Alt-F7 Prev Msg  Alt-F9 Compile  F9 Make  F10 Menu
```

Figure 3   Successful Compilation Message

Once you attempt to compile your program, one of two possible things could happen:

1)   The compiler will find no errors and will display

> **SUCCESS   :   Press any key**

and inform you that the .exe file was created.

or

2)   The compiler will find words or symbols in the source code that it does not understand and will display

> **ERRORS   :   Press any key**.

Errors denoted by the compiler are called **syntax** errors.

EXERCISE 15:   Study the following sample compiler message and indicate on the answer sheet what the computer instructs the user to do if a program contains errors.

```
  ≡  File  Edit  Search  Run  Compile Debug  Project  Options    Window  Help
 ┌[•]══════════════════════════ EXAMPLE.CPP ════════════════════════1=[↑]═┐
 │//AUTHOR:                                                              ▲
 │#include <iostream.h>                                                  ▪
 │
 │void main
 │{
 │      cout << "W┌═════════════ Compiling ═════════════┐
 │      cout << en│
 │      cout << " ║ Main file: EXAMPLE.CPP
 │      cout << en║ Compiling: EDITOR → EXAMPLE.CPP
 │      cout << " ║
 │      cout << en║                       Total    File
 │      cout << "w║ Lines compiled:       880      880
 │      cout << en║       Warnings:       0        0
 │      return;   ║         Errors:       3        3               ▼
 └═══ 4:11 ═══◄║  ║
               ║  ║ Available memory: 1937K                        ►
               ║  ║ Errors         :     Press any key
               └──└─────────────────────────────────────┘


  F1 Help  Alt-F8 Next Msg  Alt-F7 Prev Msg  Alt-F9 Compile  F9 Make  F10 Menu
```

Figure 4   Failure Compilation Message

If syntax errors are found, the compiler was not able to successfully compile your program. These errors need to be corrected before the .obj file can be created. Notice that the user is instructed to press any key. After you press a key, messages will appear at the bottom of the screen to aid you in correcting these errors:

```
  ≡  File  Edit  Search  Run  Compile Debug  Project  Options    Window  Help
 ┌[•]══════════════════════════ EXAMPLE.CPP ════════════════════════1=[↑]═┐
 │//AUTHOR:                                                              ▲
 │#include <iostream.h>                                                  ▪
 │
 │void main
 │{
 │      cout << "Welcome to the world";
 │      cout << endl;
 │      cout << "        of computing";
 │      cout << endl;
 │      cout << "            and";
 │      cout << endl;
 │      cout << "welcome to computer science";
 │      cout << endl;                                                    ▼
 │Error EXAMPLE.CPP 5: Size of 'main' is unknown or zero
 └═══ 5:2 ═══◄•────────────────────────────────────────────────────►─┘
 ┌─────────────────────────────── Message ──────────────────────────2──┐
 │ Compiling EXAMPLE.CPP:
 │Error EXAMPLE.CPP 5: Size of 'main' is unknown or zero
 │ Error EXAMPLE.CPP 5: Size of 'main' is unknown or zero
 │ Error EXAMPLE.CPP 5: Declaration syntax error
 └─────────────────────────────────────────────────────────────────────┘

  F1 Help  Alt-F8 Next Msg  Alt-F7 Prev Msg  Alt-F9 Compile  F9 Make  F10 Menu
```

Figure 5   Error Messages

EXERCISE 16: Observe the prompts in Figure 5 and fill in the blanks on the provided answer sheet.

  If you need help in understanding your errors, press ____.
  If you wish to look at the source document, press _____.
  If you wish to edit (make changes in) the source, press _____.
  If you wish to activate a menu selection, press _____.

EXERCISE 17: If you had no errors in your program, make a minor change in the program (omit the // in the first line of the program) and recompile so that you can practice correcting syntax errors.

Observe in Figure 5 that C++ instructs the user to hit <-- (the <ENTER> key) to edit a file. This will allow the user to edit or change the source file. The cursor will automatically move to the location of the first error in the program when the <ENTER> key is pressed.

You will note at this time, that the prompts on the bottom of the screen have changed and appear as:

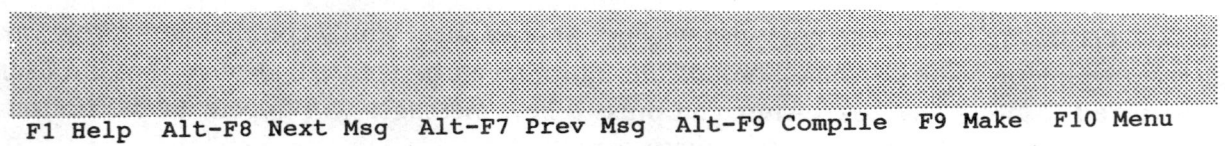

```
F1 Help   Alt-F8 Next Msg   Alt-F7 Prev Msg   Alt-F9 Compile   F9 Make   F10 Menu
```

Figure 6   Error Message Prompts

Now you may choose to be prompted for either the next or the previous error message. Also, you may choose to compile or (or make) your program now. Choose **F9** only if you are reasonably sure that you have corrected all errors.

EXERCISE 18: Begin correcting the errors in your program by hitting the <ENTER> key. Modify your code so that it is correct. Continue to edit your source file by moving the cursor to indicated errors - use the arrow keys to move the cursor.

DO NOT GO TO THE NEXT STEP UNTIL YOU HAVE SUCCESSFULLY COMPILED YOUR PROGRAM AND YOU ARE INFORMED THAT THE EXAMPLE.EXE FILE WAS CREATED!

EXERCISE 19: Let's now execute this program. Activate the word **RUN** on the menu bar and choose the word **RUN** in the pull down menu. **NOTE:** You will not see the output at this point on the screen!!

Remember that Turbo C++ works in the window environment! This means that IDE will display several windows on the screen if you so desire. Up to this point, we have been working with only one window, the file window! Now, since we have executed our .exe program, it would be desirable to see the output, right? Therefore, we need to activate the output window.

EXERCISE 20: To activate the output window, choose **WINDOW** from the menu bar and choose **OUTPUT** from the pull-down menu. If the window is not large enough for you to see your output, use the arrow keys to scroll the output screen. Briefly describe the output that you see on the screen at this time.

Before we continue, we need to learn about IDE's available window operations which will be very helpful in editing C++ files and viewing the output from a program. Study the following chart to learn how to manipulate Turbo's IDE window environment:

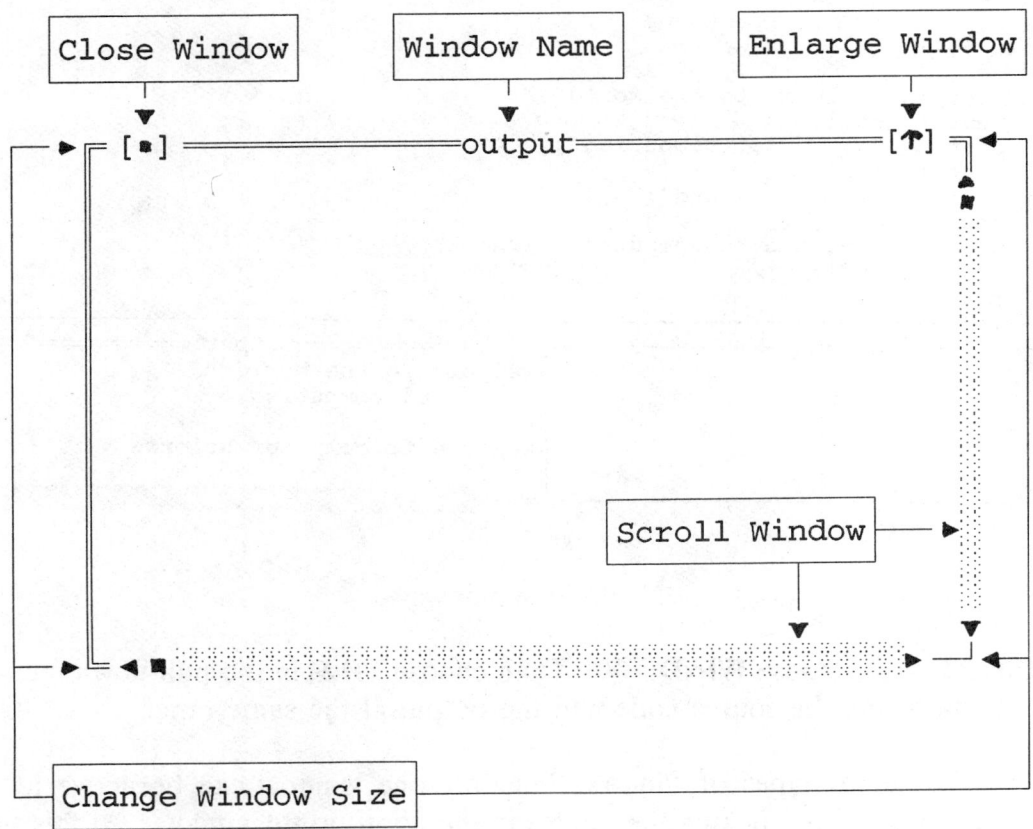

Figure 7   Window Manipulation

Note that the size and location of the windows may be changed by performing a "click and drag" of the mouse. "Click and drag" means that after you have positioned the mouse cursor at an appropriate location on the screen, you should press and hold the left mouse button while moving the mouse. If we click the mouse cursor on the top bar of a window and then drag the cursor in an upward direction, the window will move higher on the screen. Similarly, if we click and drag the mouse cursor down, the window will move lower on the screen. If we click and drag the lower right corner of a window, the size or shape of the window can be changed.

EXERCISE 21: Study Figure 7 and explain how to **quickly** close a window.

Multiple windows may also be used in the IDE environment. For example, often it is desirable to see both the source code and the output simultaneously as in Figure 8.

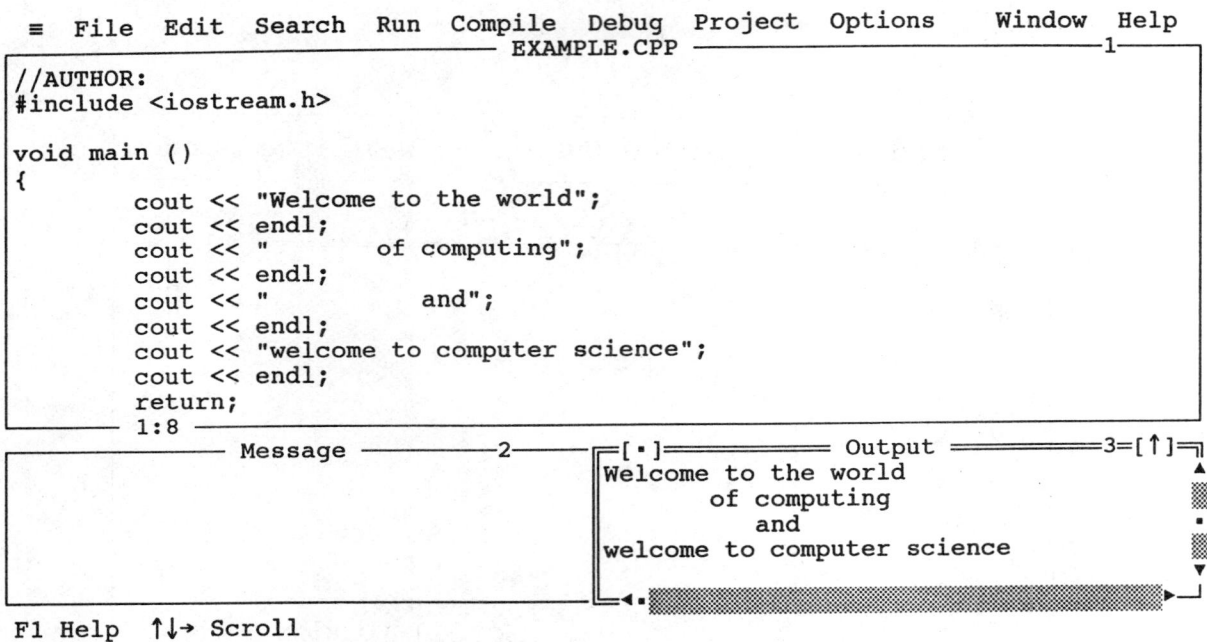

Figure 8   Multiple Windows

EXERCISE 22:   Choose **WINDOW** . Then choose **TILE** in the pull-down menu. This will enable you to see the source code and the output at the same time.

Turbo C++ has many types of windows but only one window can be active at a time. Windows are activated by clicking the mouse in the appropriate window. At this time you should see two windows on the screen: the source window and the output window. If you do not see these two windows, repeat **Exercise 22**. We will refer to these windows as the output window and the source window. The source window needs to be active when creating, editing, compiling, linking and executing your file.

EXERCISE 23:   Let's assume that you do not like the appearance of the output and that you wish to make changes in this program. Click the mouse in the source window so that this window will be active. Change the first *cout* statement so that it appears as:

    cout<<"Welcome to the wonderful world";

EXERCISE 24:   Since you have made changes in the program, you must re-compile and link the program. Press **F9** and continue to edit the program if you have errors.

EXERCISE 25:   After you have been given the success message, run this program.

EXERCISE 26:   Obtain a hardcopy (printed copy) of **example.cpp**. Remember how? Select **FILE** from the menu and then select **PRINT** from the pull-down menu!

EXERCISE 27:   Obtain a hardcopy of your output. To accomplish this:

   1)   Activate the output window (if it is not showing on the screen) by selecting **Window** and **Output.**
   2)   Select **File.**
   3)   Select **Print.**

EXERCISE 28:   Let's try moving the output window. You should see a horizontal line at the top of each window. This is called the "title bar". Position the mouse cursor on the title bar of the output window. Do not position the cursor on the ↑ included in the title bar! Practice changing the location of this window by "clicking and dragging" the mouse in different directions on the screen.

EXERCISE 29:   Close all windows. To accomplish this, select **WINDOWS** and then select **CLOSE ALL** from the pull down menu.

EXERCISE 30:   Exit IDE by selecting **FILE** and then **QUIT**. If changes were made in your source program since the last save, you will be prompted to save the changes.

Submit the answer sheet for this lab and hardcopies of **example.cpp** and **lab1.txt**. Also, submit the hardcopy of the output of **example.cpp** for grading.

NOTE: Most of the labs in this manual request hardcopies of program listings and program output. Check with your instructor to verify that these listings are required.

Congratulations on your first C++ programming experience!

Lab 1 Files

FILE: lab1.txt

We are currently in the "model - T" stage of commmuters since computers have only been around for about fifty years! Think of what that means. The power and capabilities of our present day computers will be nothing compared to their capabilities in the future. You have chosen an excellent and exciting field in entering the world of computer science. No longer do we have the days when most anyone can get satisfactory, well paying jobs without training in a particular field. These non-skilled jobs are now performed many times by robots and mankind is required to obtain some type of advanced training to acquire even minimal wage jobs. We either must learn how to use computers effectively or fall by the wayside of technology.

Congratudations on your decision to obtain knowledge in the field of programming. We use the method of programming to communicate to the computer exactly what operations we wish the computer to perform. Therefore, we must learn to program the computer to perform. Therefore, we must learn to program the computer in a particular language. The language of choice for this manual is the C++ programming language. C++ was developed by Bjarne Stroustrup and is based on Dennis Richie's C language. C++ is becoming increasingly popular outside the classroom and provides early foundational skills in modern software development.

Lab 1 - Answer Sheet

NAME: _____

EXERCISE 1: _____

_____

EXERCISE 2: _____

_____

EXERCISE 3: _____

_____

_____

EXERCISE 4: _____

_____

EXERCISE 14: _____

_____

EXERCISE 15: _____

EXERCISE 16: _____

_____

_____

_____

EXERCISE 20: _____

_____

EXERCISE 21:

Lab 2

Problem Analysis and Design

Objectives:	Introduce strategies for analyzing and solving a problem
	Introduce algorithm development

Note: You will be asked to turn in written work as well as printouts for this lab. Please use the provided answer sheets at the end of this lab to indicate all answers for the written exercises.

A. Problem Analysis and Solution

It would be nice if there were an exact foolproof recipe for solving problems. Unfortunately, there is no such recipe. Some of the strategies that we use in every day problem solving will help us to analyze programming problems. We will briefly discuss some of these strategies in this section of the lab.

Ask questions to gain an understanding of the problem.

When someone asks us to perform some task, we ask questions until what we are being asked to do is clear. We ask who, what, why, when and where. We must also ask questions when solving problems in computer science. Some questions might be:

a.   What information is given (i.e. what is my **input** data)?
b.   What does the input data look like? Is the data item an integer, a real number or a string of characters? Does the data start in a certain column of an input line?
c.   What **output** is desired?
d.   What should the output look like? Should a number have a $ in the output? Should the output appear in a certain column? Should it appear in the form of a table?
e.   What tasks (if any) need to be repeated?
f.   How do I know when I am finished with the problem?
g.   Do I have to worry about special error conditions (like division by zero or invalid input data)?

Another related question we might want to address is the best method for storing the needed data (selecting a data structure). We will address data structures briefly in this manual, but major study in this area is reserved for higher level computing classes.

Let's apply these simple questions to a problem:

EXERCISE 1:   Our Computer Science I teacher needs to determine the semester grade for 30 students. The teacher has recorded each student's name, social security number, GPA, and scores made in the class. Scores include three 100 point exams, seven 100 point lab grades and a final exam which is also 100 points. The computer science teacher says that the final grade will be determined using the percentages: 50% from the exam average, 30% from the lab average and 20% from the final exam. The teacher would like to see a table which includes a student's name, scores and final grade on each line. The teacher would also like to see the highest grade and the name of the student who made it. To gain a clear understanding of this problem, answer each of the questions below for this problem.

a)   For each student, what data is given?
b)   For each student, what must be calculated?
c)   Is there any other output requested other than information related to an individual student?
d)   In what form should the output appear?

We can also answer the question about repetition. The same set of instructions used to calculate one student's scores could be repeated for each student. Thus, we would wish to repeat that set of instructions until we had processed all 30 students.

Find a suitable solution.

Once you have gained a clear understanding of a problem, you are ready to determine a solution. Again, there is no step-by-step procedure that will lead us from an understanding of the problem to a solution. This is usually the most difficult part of problem solving.

Ask more questions!!

By asking and seeking answers to questions in Exercise 1, you already know (or have a fairly good idea about) the data to be input and the output to be produced. Thus, you can begin to establish connections between the input values and the output values by attempting to obtain a method to produce each item to be output from items that were input.

At this point, additional questions might be:

a.   If a result is to be computed from certain input values (in our problem, the semester grade is computed from input scores), what formula must you use? Is the formula clear? Are there any circumstances under which the formula is invalid?

b.   Does a result have to be computed by using a decision process? If so, what decisions must be used to obtain the result?

c.   Can each item of output be computed from the available input? If not, what additional data is needed?

EXERCISE 2:   In Exercise 1 a student had three 100 point exams, seven 100 point lab grades, and a 100 point final exam. The final grade is determined using the percentages: 50% from the exam average, 30% from the lab average, and 20% from the final exam. One item of output is the final grade. Show steps for calculating the final grade for each student.

Look at previous solutions.

In addition to asking questions when seeking to find a suitable solution, there is no need to reinvent the wheel. After we have been solving problems for a while, we will have a collection of solutions to problems which we have developed. When we encounter a new problem we may recognize that a portion of it (or all of it) can be solved using a solution which we have already developed. Thus when we attempt to solve a problem, we should look for things that are familiar.

Use divide and conquer strategies.

We often break up large problems into smaller tasks that we can solve. The task of painting a room may seem unmanageable. The individual tasks of purchasing painting supplies, preparing the room to be painted, and actually painting the room may seem more manageable. The task of purchasing painting supplies may be further refined to include the tasks of purchasing brushes, sand paper, primer, and paint. The task of purchasing the paint can be broken down further into the tasks of deciding the kind of paint to be used (enamel, flat, etc.) and deciding on the color by looking through color charts.

The same principle applies to programming. We call this strategy **top-down design**. Each successive refinement of our overall problem is called a **step-wise refinement**. In our painting problem, we could see the following refinements:

Refinement 1
1. Paint a room

Refinement 2
1. Purchase supplies
2. Prepare room to be painted
3. Paint the room

Refinement 3
1. Purchase supplies
    1.1. purchase paint brushes
    1.2. purchase sand paper
    1.3. purchase paint
2. Prepare room to be painted
    2.1. Move furniture to allow access to walls
    2.2. Remove any pictures, etc. from walls
    2.3. Fill any holes with putty
    etc.

Sometimes problems in computing have beginning refinements which may include getting input data, calculating output values and printing out the results. We will use this observation to solve the following problem.

EXERCISE 3:   Use top-down design to solve the grades problem for one student. Determine the semester grade of a student in a computer science class. Scores include three 100 point exams, seven 100 point lab grades, and a final exam which is also 100 points. The teacher says that the final grade will be determined using the percentages: 50% from the exam average, 30% from the lab average and 20% from the final exam. Beginning refinements to this problem are shown below.

Refinement 1
1. Determine the grade for one student

Refinement 2
1. Input the scores made by the student
2. Calculate the student's final grade
3. Output the scores and final grade

Show Refinement 3 for this problem. In other words, show more detail for each step in

Refinement 2 above.

Look for alternate solutions to a problem.

Many times there may be several different solutions to a problem. Suppose we are traveling to an event and when we try to start our car, we discover that we have a dead battery. We wish to start on our way as soon as possible. Some solutions to this problem might be:

1.   Call a relative or friend to come and repair the car.
2.   Call an auto mechanic and continue on our way after the battery has been charged.
3.   Leave the car and proceed on foot. Come back to repair the car later.
4.   Buy another car and drive to our destination.

Some solutions can be rejected immediately as unsuitable, say number 4. However, the choice of the most "suitable" solution may depend on the circumstances. For example, if we are very close to our destination and we are required to arrive quickly, number 3 might be chosen.

B.   Developing an Algorithm

Once we have analyzed our problem and broken it into subproblems which we can solve, we wish to develop an algorithm to portray the solution to the problem. An algorithm is to a computer programmer as a blueprint is to a housebuilder. Just as a good builder would not attempt to build a house without blueprints, neither should a good programmer attempt to write a program without designing an algorithm first.

What is an algorithm? An **algorithm** is a finite sequence of effective statements that, when applied to the problem, will solve it. Let us consider the characteristics of an algorithm.

1.   _An algorithm must work._ This simply means that the algorithm should solve the problem it is supposed to solve.
2.   _An algorithm must be finite_. That is, it must eventually stop.
3.   _An algorithm consists of effective statements._ This means that each of the steps must be described in such a clear and unambiguous way that it can be performed easily by carrying out the steps.
4.   _An algorithm should be as general as possible._ This means that the procedure should not be so limited that it solves the problem only for one specific case. Instead, it should be capable of producing solutions for a variety of cases.

EXERCISE 4:   Consider the following. Decide whether each is an **appropriate** algorithm to solve the given problem. **Tell why or why not.**

A.   Purpose: To find the area of a room in square feet.

　　　Step 1.　　　Get the length and width of the room in feet.
　　　Step 2.　　　Area = length + width
　　　Step 3.　　　Output the area

B.　　Purpose:　　Find the real number solutions to $Ax^2 + Bx + C = 0$. Assume that A
　　　　　　　　is not zero.

　　　Step 1.　　　Get values for A, B, C
　　　Step 2.　　　IF $B^2 - 4AC$ is greater than or equal zero THEN calculate x1 and x2
　　　　　　　　where:

$$x1 = \frac{-B + \sqrt{B^2 - 4AC}}{2A}$$

　　　　　　and

$$x2 = \frac{-B - \sqrt{B^2 - 4AC}}{2A}$$
　　　　　　and output the results

　　　　　　　ELSE
　　　　　　　　　indicate that there is no real number solution
　　　Step 3.　　　Output x1 and x2

C.   Purpose: Water a plant

　　　Step 1. Buy a can of plant food
　　　Step 2. Read the directions on the can
　　　Step 3. Add indicated amount of plant food to indicated amount of water
　　　Step 4. When the plant needs water, water it with the mixture made up in step 3.

C. Components of Algorithms

In addition to identifying an algorithm's characteristics, it is helpful to define a set of basic components that serve as building blocks for any algorithm. Familiarity with these building blocks makes it much easier to design and develop algorithms, so that their conversion to reliable programs becomes as simple as possible. We will express our algorithms in **pseudocode** (an English like representation) and we will present our building blocks in pseudocode.

The basic building blocks of an algorithm using pseudocode include:

1.   **The sequence**--The simplest activity is a succession of tasks, one after the other. The following set of tasks is a sequence:

Step 1.   Read the number of hours worked and the rate of pay per hour for an employee.
Step 2.   Compute the employee's pay.
Step 3.   Display the employee's rate of pay, hours worked, and pay.

Each of the steps, when examined further, may itself turn out to be a sequence. As a further example, consider our top-down design for painting a room. Each refinement consisted of a sequence of statements.

2.   **Decision**--Not all activities can be expressed as a sequence. Algorithms often make a decision between two activities depending on the outcome of some test. This process is usually called the IF-THEN-ELSE structure. Its basic description is as follows:

IF the condition is true
        perform this activity (or these activities)
ELSE (if the condition is false)
        perform a second activity (or activities) instead.

We have such a structure in the example above. Look more closely at step 2 in our pay problem above. Computing an employee's pay could involve the decision process. If the employee worked overtime, let us assume that the rate of pay is one and a half times the normal rate. Using the decision structure, step 2 could be rewritten as follows:

IF hours worked is less than or equal 40
        Pay = rate * hours worked
ELSE
        Pay = rate * 40 + (hours worked - 40) * 1.5 * rate

3.   **Repetition**--The third component of an algorithm is a loop, a process in which an activity may be performed over and over making sure the process does not repeat endlessly. There are several ways to achieve such a loop. The one we shall discuss is known as the **WHILE** structure. This loop's activity consists of four basic steps that we can describe as follows:

Step 1.   Prepare a test that will control the loop's processing to be performed. This is called initializing the loop.
Step 2.   Perform the test set up in Step 1. It will produce one of two possible outcomes:

If the outcome is true
>   proceed with Step 3
ELSE
>   skip Steps 3 and 4 and exit the loop. That is, quit the loop and
>   continue with a statement outside the loop.

Step 3.   Perform whatever action it is that forms the body of the loop.
Step 4.   Return to step 2.

We can't say anything specific about the processing performed in Step 3. However, it must include some action that will eventually change the outcome of the test in Step 2 and cause the loop to be exited. Remember our algorithm must be finite.

This algorithmic component is called a **WHILE** structure because it is saying, "keep performing the processing in the loop while the test is true." As an example of how this works, let's expand our problem. We will now read information about an employee consisting of hours worked, rate of pay per hour, and an ID number for the employee. We will compute pay and print a pay check for each employee until an ID is read for an employee which is negative (< 0). A negative ID will be like a flag saying that we are done processing employees. The pseudocode solution to this problem might be:

Step 1.   get the first employee ID (this sets up the test!)
Step 2.   (the test is next)
               WHILE the ID is greater than or equal to 0
Step 3.   (here comes the statements to be repeated)
               (3.1)   Read in the hours worked and rate of pay
               (3.2)   IF hours worked is less than or equal 40
                           Pay = rate * hours worked
                       ELSE
                           Pay = rate * 40 + (hours worked - 40) * 1.5 * rate
               (3.3)   output the ID, hours worked, rate of pay, and salary
               (3.4)   read in the next ID
Step 4.   RETURN: go back to step 2.

An **ENDWHILE** statement may be used to replace step 4 above. Thus using the ENDWHILE, our final pseudocode might appear as:

get the first employee ID
WHILE the ID is greater than or equal to 0
>   Read in the hours worked and rate

> **IF** hours worked is less than or equal 40
>> Pay = rate * hours worked
>
> **ELSE**
>> Pay = rate * 40 + (hours worked - 40) * 1.5 * rate
>
> output the ID, hours worked, rate, and salary
> read in the next ID
>
> **ENDWHILE**

Once we have completed an algorithm's pseudocode description, we are ready to express our solution as a sequence of program statements to be performed by a computer. If our algorithm design was reasonable, this part of the process will simply be a translation from one language to another.

Develop an algorithm and type in a pseudocode description for the following problems. You may use Turbo's IDE editor or any available word processing software. Turn in a printout of the typed algorithms to your lab instructor.

EXERCISE 5: The problem of paying a bill by check through the mail. (Specify as many steps as possible--determine the amount to be paid, determine your balance, decide whether you have enough money, write the check, etc.)

EXERCISE 6: Expand Exercise 5 above and use a loop to pay all of your monthly bills (telephone, electric, water, rent, etc.)

EXERCISE 7: Many states base the cost of car registration on the weight of the vehicle. Suppose the fees are as follows:

Weight	Cost
up to 2,000	25.00
over 2,000 pounds	50.00

Write an algorithm which when given the weight of a car, finds and prints the cost of registration.

EXERCISE 8: Expand Exercise 7 above and use a loop to continue to process cars until a negative number is input for the weight of the car.

Lab 2 - Answer Sheet

NAME: _____

EXERCISE 1:

   a) _____

   _____

   _____

   b) _____

   _____

   _____

   c) _____

   _____

   _____

   d) _____

   _____

   _____

EXERCISE 2:

EXERCISE 3:

      Refinement 3:

EXERCISE 4:

    A.

    B.

    C.

Lab 3

C++ Input, Output, and Simple Data Types

Objectives:	Learn to use integer, real and character constants and variables.
	Learn operations which can be used with integer and real expressions.
	Practice using assignment statements.
	Learn to use standard input and output functions - cin and cout.

In Lab 2, we learned how to analyze a problem and how to design a solution for it. Our next step is to learn some C++ basics so that we can implment a design as a program written in the C++ language.

To implement and design a program, we must first learn how to perform certain tasks in the language we are using.

A.   Constants and Variables

In order to work with data, we must place it in memory. In C++, a variable or a constant is used to accomplish this. A **variable** is a symbolic name used to refer to a memory location in which data is stored. The data in this type of memory location may vary. A **constant** is a symbolic name used to refer to a memory location in which the data stays constant. When we wish to place a value into a memory location during program execution, we use the symbolic name for that memory location. In C++, a symbolic name is a word which begins with a letter followed by any combination of 127 or less characters composed of letters, digits, and the underscore.

31

For example, *sum, x, product, r2d2, a1, fairlylongname, and hours_worked* are all acceptable names. Unacceptable names include *4thofjuly, x-axis, and c++*. C++ does distinguish between upper and lower case letters. *SUM, Sum*, and *sum* all refer to different memory locations.

One should choose names which resemble what they represent. That is, use *rateofpay* to represent a person's rate of pay per hour.

C++ has special words, called **reserved words**, which have a specific meaning unique to C++. These words cannot be used for other purposes and thus, can not be used as symbolic names. Look in your C++ textbook for a complete list of all reserved words. A few of these words are *float, int, main, char*.

EXERCISE 1:   Indicate whether each of the following are valid or invalid names for constants or variables. If invalid, explain why they can't be used.

> a) average
> b) thisisalongname
> c) howlongistoolong?
> d) 3rd
> e) float
> f) length_in_sqft

B. Numeric Data Types

Once we know what values we wish to store and have chosen names for them, we must decide what type of data will be placed in memory. We must also decide whether the value will change or stay constant. We may also wish to perform calculations on the values. Therefore, we must be aware of the operations that can be performed on various data types.

Our first data type is the **integer** data type. When we tell C++ that a variable is an integer type, we are restricting the type of data that can be stored in the variable to an integer. Therefore, only whole numbers (-50, 2, 1000, and 0 are examples) can be stored in this memory location. The size of the integer is limited by the computer's architecture.

To declare the variables *count* and *numitems* to be integer variables, we use the C++ variable declaration statement:

> *int count, numitems;*

Note the semicolon at the end of the above C++ statement. It is required.

To declare the integer constant *hours_per_day* to contain the value 24, we use the C++ statement:

$$const\ int\ hours\_per\_day = 24;$$

Notice that this declaration is very similar to the declaration of a variable. In the above example, however, the C++ reserved word *const* makes the name refer to a location which will not change and the value 24 is placed in that memory location.

A second type of data that can be stored in a memory location is the **float** type which may contain real numbers, or numbers that have a decimal point like 3.5, -.0048, or 12.5896. A real (floating point) number may use an *e* to indicate the number should be multiplied by powers of ten. The number 2.75 can be represented by any of the following:
2.75e0, .275e1, 27.5e-1, etc.
where $2.75e0 = 2.75 \times 10^0$, $.275e1 = .275 \times 10^1$, etc.

To declare the constant *pi* to contain 3.14159 and the variables *radius* and *area* to contain real values, the C++ reserved word *float* is used.

$$const\ float\ pi = 3.14159;$$
$$float\ radius,\ area;$$

EXERCISE 2:   Show C++ statements to declare the variable *quarter* to be a constant which contains the value 25, the variables *age* and *weight* to be integer variables and the variable *length* to be a float variable.

C. Numeric Operators

Operators that may be used on numeric data include:

Operator		Integer example	Real example
+	Add	2 + 3 is 5	3.56 + 4.01 is 7.57
-	Subtract	4 - 1 is 3	8.45 - 10.3 is -1.85
*	Multiply	4 * 3 is 12	0.2 * 100.0 is 20.0
/	Divide	20 / 6 is 3	2.68 / 2.0 is 1.34
%	Modulus	20 % 6 is 2	% is not valid for real numbers

There are no surprises in this table except for how the / and % operators treat integer data. When we divide one integer by another integer, we can obtain a quotient and a remainder using the / and % operators.

In our example:

```
              3    <---------Quotient or 20 / 6
         6 | 20
           18
                   _____
              2    <---------Remainder or 20 % 6
```

EXERCISE 3:   Evaluate the following:

   a. 5 * 6   b. 18 / 5   c. 5 / 6   d. 18 % 5   e. 5 % 6

If there are more than one operators in an expression, we use the following rules to decide which operator will be performed first:

   1. All parenthesized expressions are evaluated first.
   2. The operators *, /, and % are performed next.
   3. The operators + and - are performed last.

If there are more than one of the operators *, /, or % in an expression, then the leftmost operator is performed first. Similarly if there are more than one of the operators + and - in an expression, then they are performed from left to right.

For example:

   3 * 2 * (13 / 3) + 2 = 3 * 2 * 4 + 2   parentheses first
                        = 6 * 4 + 2   * next (left-most)
                        = 24 + 2   * next
                        = 26   + last

EXERCISE 4:   Evaluate:

   a) 2 + 3 * 4 - 5
   b) 14 % 8 / 2
   c) 17 * ((3 - 1) / 7)
   d) 2.0 + 3.0 * (2.0 - 6.0 / 4.0)

D. Assignment Statement

Now that we know how to set up memory locations, what type of data can be placed in memory locations, and what types of arithmetic operations can be performed on each type of data, we need to know how to place data into a variable memory location. We will accomplish this by using the assignment statement or by using the C++ *cin* statement.

A value may be placed into a memory location with an assignment statement which has the form:

$$variable\_name = expression;$$

where the expression is always evaluated first, then the resulting value is assigned to the variable. Note that this value replaces any "old" value that the variable may have had. For example, the assignment:

$$age = 21;$$

gives the variable *age* the value 21. If the next statement is:

$$age = age * 2;$$

then 21 is replaced with 42.

Note: The data types of the variable on the left and the expression on the right should agree. It would not be proper to use:

$$age = 21.5;$$

Mathematical expressions and equations can be converted to C++ by using the operators and operator priorities discussed above. Care must be taken to make sure that the operations with highest priority are done first. For example, to convert the following mathematical expression to C++,

$$\frac{2A + B}{CD}$$

note that the numerator and denominator must be completely evaluated before the division can take place. Thus both must be enclosed in parentheses. The resulting C++ expression is:

$$(2*A + B)/(C*D)$$

EXERCISE 5:   Write assignment statements for the following:

a) A = 1/3 bh

b) $E = J (J + 1) h^2 / 8$

c) Place the average of the values in t1, t2, and t3 into the variable *average*.

E. C++ Input/Output Statements

The second method we will use to place values into a variable is by using the *cin* statement to input values from the standard input device (usually the keyboard). For example:

cin >> age >> weight;

requests values for age and weight to be typed at the keyboard. The input values must be separated by one or more blanks. The input operator >> skips any blanks that separate data items.

To place the results of computations or the current contents of a memory location on the standard output device (usually the screen), we use the C++ statement *cout*. For example:

cout << "Your age is " << age << endl;

displays two items; the character string "Your age is" and the value of *age*. A string is a sequence of characters enclosed in double quotes; the characters inside the quotes will be printed but the quotes will not be printed. If *age* contained the value 21, then the output would appear as:

Your age is 21

EXERCISE 6:   Look at the C++ program *inlab3a.cpp* on your lab disk. The program solves the problem of entering data for a landlord who owns an apartment and wishes to know what his earnings are. The data to be entered include the rent per month and the number of months rented. The variables for these two values are *rent* and *num_months*. The landlord has hired an overseer to take care of the apartment who receives a commission of 5% of the earnings from the apartment. Since this is a constant rate, the constant *rate* has been chosen to hold this data. Assignment statements have been used to place values in the variables *rent* and *num_months*.

a) Compile and run this program after you have looked at it and made sure that you understand it. Describe the output generated by this program on the provided answer sheet.

b) Instead of assignment statements, we wish to enter values for *rent* and *num_months* from the keyboard. Modify the program so that the assignment statements are replaced by an appropriate input statement. Immediately before the input statement, place an output statement which prints the string:

Please enter the rent/month and the number of months:

After you have modified your program, recompile and run it again. Turn in a printout of the changed program.

F. Character Data Type

In addition to numeric data, character data may be placed in memory. To declare a variable which can contain a single character value, use the C++ reserved word *char*. Suppose we wished to declare the variables *initial1* and *initial2* to contain any single character value. We would use:

> *char initial1, initial2;*

Values could be placed into the variables using assignment statements or *cin*.

> *initial1 = 'J';*
> *initial2 = 'K';*

places the characters *J* and *K* into the two variables respectively. Note that a single character is denoted by surrounding the character with apostrophes. Alternately, the following will accomplish the same thing:

> *cout << "Please enter your initials: ";*
> *cin >> initial1 >> initial2;*

If we executed these instructions, the data could be entered in either of the following ways:

> Please enter your initials: JK
> or
> Please enter your initials: J K
> or
> Please enter your initials: J
> K

Blanks, tabs and carriage returns are ignored on input!

EXERCISE 7:   In our problem in Exercise 6, suppose that the landlord wishes to have the initials of the person renting his apartment printed as well as the earnings of the apartment. Look at the C++ program *inlab3b.cpp* on your disk. This program reads the initials of the person renting the apartment, the rent per month, and the number of months the apartment has been rented. It then prints out the earnings. Run the program and when it asks for input, enter your initials. Run the program several times - once with the initials all together, once with one or more blanks between initials, and once with commas between initials (to see what happens when you goof)! Describe the output on the provided answer sheet.

Lab 3 Files

```
//File:          inlab3a.cpp
//Author:
//Purpose:       This program calculates a landlord's earnings
//               on an apartment given the rent per month, the
//               number of months rented and a deduction of 5%
//               commission for an overseer.

//include files...
#include <iostream.h>

void main()
{
    //variable and constant declarations...
    const float rate = 0.05;        // overseer's commission rate
    float rent;                     // rent per month
    float num_months;               // number of months rented
    float earnings;                 // earnings on the apartment

    //assign values for rent per month and number of months
    rent = 250;
    num_months = 7;

    //calculate earnings
    earnings = (1.0 - rate) * rent * num_months;

    // display results
    cout << endl;
    cout << "The rent per month is: " << rent << endl;
    cout << "The apartment has been rented for ";
    cout << num_months << " months." <<endl;
    cout << "The overseer receives a " << 100 * rate;
    cout << "% commission rate. " << endl;
    cout << "The earnings were: " << earnings << endl;

    //end of main...
    return;
}
```

```
//File:          inlab3b.cpp
//Author:
//Purpose:       This program calculates a landlord's earnings
//               on an apartment given the rent per month, the
//               number of months rented and a deduction of 5%
//               commission for an overseer.  Initials for the
//               apartment renter are also input.

//include files...
#include <iostream.h>

void main()
{
    //variable and constant declarations...
    const float rate = 0.05;        // overseer's commission rate
    float rent;                     // rent per month
    float num_months;               // number of months rented
    float earnings;                 // earnings on the apartment
    char initial1,
         initial2,
         initial3;                  // initials of the apartment renter

    //input apartment renter, rent/month and number of months
    //the apartment has been rented.
    cout << endl;
    cout << "Please enter the renter's initials (first middle last): ";
    cin  >> initial1 >> initial2 >> initial3;
    cout << "Now enter the rent per month and the number of months: ";
    cin  >> rent >> num_months;

    //calculate earnings
    earnings = (1.0 - rate) * rent * num_months;

    // display results
    cout << endl << endl;
    cout << "The initials of the apartment renter are: ";
    cout << initial1 << initial2 << initial3 << endl;
    cout << "The rent per month is: " << rent << endl;
    cout << "The apartment has been rented for ";
    cout << num_months << " months." <<endl;
    cout << "The overseer receives a " << 100 * rate;
    cout << "% commission rate. " << endl;
    cout << "The earnings were: " << earnings << endl;

    //end of main...
    return;
}
```

Lab 3 - Answer Sheet

NAME: _____

EXERCISE 1:

    a) _____

    b) _____

    c) _____

    d) _____

    e) _____

    f) _____

EXERCISE 2:

    _____

    _____

    _____

EXERCISE 3:

    a) _____

    b) _____

    c) _____

    d) _____

    e) _____

EXERCISE 4:

    a) _____

    b) _____

    c) _____

    d) _____

EXERCISE 5:

    a) _____

    b) _____

    c) _____

EXERCISE 6:

    a)

EXERCISE 7:

Lab 4

Modularity and C++ Functions

Objectives:	Review top-down design and modularity
	Introduce C++ functions

A. Review of Top Down Design

One of the major problems in the development of a large software system is that of controlling the complexity of the system. One method for managing this complexity is to divide the problem into smaller sub-problems which are more easily understood and solved. This type of design method is called top-down design as we discussed in Lab 2. Therefore, if a computer scientist has been given a complex problem to solve, the solution could be broken up into several parts where each part performs **one** particular task. If a program is written in this fashion, we say that the program is "modular" and each of the divisions or parts are called **modules**. Consider the following problem:

> The math teacher, Mrs. Jones, needs a program which will produce a letter for the parents of each student in her class. She would like for the letter to explain her grading policies. She also wants the letter to contain the test grades and the test average for the student. Finally, the letter should tell the parents whether the student's work is passing or failing.

To solve this problem for one student, we could use top-down design. Our first refinement might appear as:

1.   Get grades for one student
2.   Print a heading explaining Mrs. Jones' grading policies
3.   Calculate the average for this student
4.   Print this student's grades and their status (Pass/Fail)

Each of these steps may be thought of as a single task which must be performed in the specified order, to solve the problem for a given student. We can divide this problem into the following modules:

1- MODULE 1:   **GetGrades**
    PURPOSE: Obtain all data related to a student in Mrs. Jones' mathematics class.

2- MODULE 2:   **PrintHeading**
    PURPOSE: Print a greeting and a message concerning Mrs. Jones' grading policies.

3- MODULE 3:   **Average**
    PURPOSE: Calculate the test average for a student.

4- MODULE 4:   **PrintGrades**
    PURPOSE: Print out the test grades, the test average for the student and indicate whether or not the student is passing.

The following observations about modules should be noted at this time:

1)   A module should have a single purpose.
2)   A module should have a name related to its purpose.
3)   The number of modules needed to solve a problem depends on the complexity of the problem.
4)   Each module should be fairly simple. A rule of thumb often used is that the code for a module should not exceed one page in length.

EXERCISE 1:   Give appropriate modules which might be used to allow the user to input three numbers representing the three sides of a triangle and print a message explaining whether the triangle is equilateral (all sides are the same), isosceles (two sides are equal) or scalene (all sides are different). **Remember, do not write a program!** Name the modules and tell the purpose of each.

When we have a problem to solve, we can use top-down design to find a solution to the problem. The use of top-down design will result in the creation of several modules which collectively will exhibit a solution to the original problem. The following strategy in writing C++ modular programs should be observed:

1) After understanding the details of the problem (analyzing the problem), use top-down design to divide the problem into separate, concise modules.
2) For each module, develop pseudocode to solve the desired task.
3) Write a C++ main module which will call each of the separate modules to solve the problem.
4) Translate each separate module into C++.

Now, we consider how to translate the modules we have written to C++.

B. C++ FUNCTIONS

C++ possesses a construct, called a *function*, which will allow us to write modular programs. A function is a specific grouping of statements which performs a specified task. A modular solution to a particular problem, then, will consist of one or more functions which collaborate to solve the given problem.

Before we proceed further, observe the following C++ program called **inlab4a.cpp**. NOTE: Do not be unduly alarmed if you do not completely understand all parts of this program - you are not expected to!!

```
1    //File:        inlab4a.cpp
2    //Author:
3    //Purpose:     This program allows the user to input three test
4    //             scores interactively.  It then prints the scores
5    //             and the final average of the student.
6
7    //include files...
8    #include <iostream.h>
9    #include <iomanip.h>
10
11   void main ()
12   {
13       //function prototypes....
14       void print_heading ();               //print a school heading
15       void print_intro ();                 //print introductory message
16       void print_stars ();                 //print a line of stars
17       float average (int, int, int);       //compute average
18       void print_grades (int, int, int, float);   //display results
19
20       //local variables...
21       int grade1, grade2, grade3;          //student scores
22       float final;                         //final average
23
24       //display the school heading and introductory message
25       print_heading ();
26       print_stars ();
```

```
27          print_intro ();
28          print_stars ();
29
30          //input the student's scores
31          cout << "Enter the grades for test 1, test 2 ";
32          cout << "and test 3."<< endl;
33          cout <<"Then, press <ENTER>." << endl;
34          cin   >> grade1 >> grade2 >> grade3;
35
36          //find the average
37          final = average (grade1, grade2, grade3);
38
39          //display the results
40          print_grades (grade1, grade2, grade3, final);
41          print_stars ();
42
43          //end of main...
44          return;
45      }
46
47
48      //Function:      print_heading()
49      //Purpose:       Print the school heading.
50
51      void print_heading ()
52      {
53          cout <<"            ONE TIME SCHOOL" << endl;
54          cout <<"         SOMEWHERE, IN SOMESTATE" << endl;
55          cout <<"   NATIONAL CHAMPS IN THE WORLD CONTEST" << endl;
56          return;
57      }
58
59
60      //Function:      print_stars()
61      //Purpose:       Print a line of stars.
62
63      void print_stars ()
64      {
65          cout <<"*****************************************************",
66          cout << endl;
67          return;
68      }
69
70
71      //Function:      average()
72      //Purpose:       Compute the average of three test grades.
73
74      float average ( int test1, int test2, int test3)          //IN: three test grades
75      {
76          return (test1 + test2 + test3)/3;
77      }
```

```
78      //Function:      print_grades()
79      //Purpose:       Print three test grades and their average.
80
81      void print_grades (int grade1,
82                         int grade2,
83                         int grade3,     //IN: three test grades
84                         float final)    //IN: final average of the grades
85
86      {
87          cout << endl;
88          cout << endl;
89          cout <<"TEST 1 grade is:" << setw (7) << grade1 << endl;
90          cout <<"TEST 2 grade is:" << setw (7) << grade2 << endl;
91          cout <<"TEST 3 grade is:" << setw (7) << grade3 << endl;
92          cout <<"_____" << endl;
93          cout << endl;
94          cout <<"AVERAGE IS:" << setw (7) << final << endl;
95          cout << endl;
96          cout << endl;
97          return;
98      }
99
100
101     //Function:      print_intro()
102     //Purpose:       Print an introduction to the program.
103
104     void print_intro ()
105     {
106         cout << "Welcome to the TEST program." << endl << endl;
107         cout << "This program will allow the user to enter three ";
108         cout << "test grades."<<endl;
109         cout << "A chart will then be printed indicating:"<< endl;
110         cout << "1:  ALL TEST GRADES" << endl;
111         cout << "2:  AVERAGE OF TESTS" << endl;
112         cout << endl;
113         return;
114     }
```

This program presents some very important facts related to C++ programming. These facts are:

a) **A C++ program consists of a collection of one or more functions.** The above program is a modular program which consists of exactly six functions.

b) **Each function in a C++ program must have a name associated with it.** In the above example, the names of the functions are: main, print_heading, print_stars, average, print_grades, and print_intro.

c) **Functions may or may not return a value using the *return* statement.** Sometimes the purpose of a function is to compute a value. For example, notice on line #76 of the above program that the function called *average* has a return statement which actually returns the average of the three tests. Also, observe line #67. Here we see that the function *print_stars()* does not return a value using the return statement.

d)   **Every C++ program must contain a special function called *main*.**

e)   **The primary purpose of the function called *main* is to activate (cause to be executed) other functions in the program.**

f)   **The *main* function is always executed first in a C++ program no matter where the *main* function physically resides in the program.**

g)   **Some functions have input arguments while others do not. Input arguments are used to send values to a function from the calling function. Notice that the function *average* has three integer arguments (see line #74). Since this function computes the average of three numbers, we need to "send" these values to this function and we call these values, input arguments. Note that the function *print_intro* (see line #104) does not have arguments since no values are needed in this function.**

h)   **Each function SHOULD accomplish a single well defined task.** Examine the above functions and the purpose for each function.

FUNCTION	PURPOSE
main	input values for the three test grades and activate all remaining functions in the order required to solve the problem.
print_grades	print out all test grades and the average of all of the tests.
average	compute the average of the three tests and return this value to the function *main*.
print_intro	print out a description of the program.
print_heading	print school heading
print_stars	print a row of stars to decorate output

EXERCISE 2: Load the file **inlab4b.cpp** and answer the following questions on the provided answer sheet:

a) How many functions are contained in this program?
b) What are the names of all functions contained in this program?
c) What is the purpose for each function?

Hopefully, you realized by reading the above material that there are several different categories of functions: functions with return values, functions with no return value, functions with input arguments, etc . For the remainder of this lab, we will concentrate on one type of function: functions with no arguments and with no return values. Future labs will be devoted to more complex functions.

C. Function Syntax

Now, let's consider the basic guidelines for creating all C++ functions. There are three basic things to remember when writing C++ functions. All C++ functions (except for the function called *main*) **MUST** be:

a) **Declared,**
b) **Activated and**
c) **Defined.**

All we need to remember is DAD!

FUNCTION DECLARATION

Previously, we learned that the C++ compiler requires specific information related to all variables which will be used in the C++ program. The compiler also requires specific information related to all functions called in the program. To provide this information to the compiler, we must use a function declaration statement (function prototype). The syntax for the function prototype is:

type function name (formal argument type list);

Consider the following example of a function prototype:

void printout ();

This function prototype gives the following information to the compiler concerning the *printout* () function:

1)   a function called *printout* will be used by this program.
2)   the function *printout* () requires no arguments. This is indicated by the empty parentheses () following the name of the function in the prototype.
3)   this function will not compute or return a value. This is indicated by the word *void* preceding the name of the function.

EXERCISE 3:   Note the placement of the function prototypes in the program **inlab4a.cpp** and describe by indicating appropriate line numbers where the prototypes are located in this C++ program. On the answer sheet, indicate the name of each function and the line number of its function prototype.

EXERCISE 4:   One last observation in regard to function prototypes relates to the placement of comments. To aid in the readability of C++ programs, it is often suggested that comments be placed beside a function prototype, indicating what task the particular function performs. Using **inlab4a.cpp** as an example, load **inlab4b.cpp** and insert appropriate function comments.

FUNCTION ACTIVATION

No function in a C++ program will be executed unless it is "activated" or "called" by another function. Study the following lines from **inlab4a.cpp** in the function *main*:

```
print_intro ();
final = average (grade1, grade2, grade3);
print_grades (grade1, grade2, grade3, final);
```

As you can see there are two basic ways to call a function:

1)   To activate the function *print_intro*, we merely need to specify the name of the function and use () to indicate that the function requires no arguments. To call the function *print_grades*, we specify the name of the function and provide the actual input arguments.

2)   To activate the function *average*, we must remember that this function computes a value and returns a value to the calling function. This is also indicated by the function prototype. Therefore, we must activate or call this function in a different manner. Note in this case, we have used an assignment statement and must list the values to be sent to the function in the argument list. In this example, when the function value is returned, it is placed in the variable *final*.

EXERCISE 5: Consider **inlab4b.cpp**. Determine which statements activate the functions in this C++ program. Write these activation statements on the answer sheet.

FUNCTION DEFINITION

The function definition is a listing of the actual steps that should be executed in the function. For example, if we had a function called *print_heading,* we would assume that the definition for that function would contain several output statements until an appropriate heading had been output.

The function definition is composed of two separate divisions:
a function *header* and a function *body*.

The function header appears as:
type function name (formal argument list)

Observe the following example function header:
void print_stars ()

NOTE 1: The function header **DOES NOT** end with a semicolon!
NOTE 2: The function header **closely** resembles the function prototype!

The function body appears as follows:

```
{
    [local declarations];  // a phrase in [] means "optional"
    executable statements;
    return [value];
}
```

Note that the function body:

1)	requires a { at the beginning.
2)	requires a } at the end.
3)	may or may not require local declarations. If variables are needed in the function, then these variables should be declared at the beginning of the function body.
4)	always ends with the word *return* and the value to be returned if there is one. This tells the compiler to return control to the function that activated this function and to return the calculated value (if one is returned) to the point of the call.

EXERCISE 6:   Continue working with the **inlab4b.cpp** program and add a function to this program. Call the function *print_initials*. This function should "draw" your initials using block letters similar to the following design.

```
**   **     ********
**   **     **    **
******      ********
**   **     **
**   **     **
```

Don't forget DAD when you are adding this function! All functions must be **Declared, Activated and Defined!**

EXERCISE 7:   Redesign the *main* function so that the appropriate functions are activated to create a decorative design (draw a multi-level house, rocket ship, trees, etc.). Be sure to call the functions in *main* and, please remember that functions may be called more than one time, if so desired.

EXERCISE 8:   Work on your programming style and place appropriate comments in this program. Be sure that:
1)   appropriate comments appear before each function prototype;
2)   blank lines are used to separate functions;
3)   place comments immediately preceding each function definition and explain the purpose of the indicated function; and
4)   insert your name, class and teacher in the beginning of the program.

EXERCISE 9: Compile and execute this program. Turn in a listing and run of this program.

Lab 4 Files

```cpp
//File:          inlab4b.cpp
//Author:

#include <iostream.h>

void main ()
{
    void print_parallel ();
    void print_intersecting ();
    void print_horizonal ();

    print_intersecting ();
    print_horizonal ();
    print_parallel ();
    print_horizonal ();

    return;

}

void print_parallel ()
{
    cout << "¦              ¦" << endl;
    cout << "¦              ¦" << endl;
    cout << "¦              ¦" << endl;
    cout << "¦              ¦" << endl;
    cout << "¦              ¦" << endl;
    return;
}

void print_intersecting ()
{
    cout << "        *        " << endl;
    cout << "      *   *      " << endl;
    cout << "    *       *    " << endl;
    cout << "  *           *  " << endl;
    cout << " *             * " << endl;
    cout <<"*               *" << endl;
}

void print_horizonal ()
{
    cout << "--------------------" << endl;
    return;
}
```

Lab 4 - Answer Sheet

NAME:_____

EXERCISE 1:

EXERCISE 2:

    a) _____

    b) _____

    c) _____

EXERCISE 3:

EXERCISE 5:

Lab 5

User Defined and Library Functions

Objectives:	To learn advantages for using C++ functions
	To introduce common library functions
	To discuss functions with input arguments
	To study user-defined functions

A.   Advantages of C++ Functions

We saw in Lab 4 that the use of top-down design can help to reduce the complexity of a large program. In that lab, we divided a large problem into smaller modules, each of which had a single purpose.   After the design phase, these modules were translated into C++ functions. We concluded that the use of functions aided in obtaining the solution of a large, complex program by allowing the designer to write code for smaller, less complicated modules (functions). Other benefits of using C++ functions include:

1)   Once a function has been written and included in a C++ program, the function may be called several times. If you refer back to *inlab4a.cpp* from Lab 4 you will recall that the function *print_stars()* was called several times. Therefore, we see that by using a function we were able to reduce the size of our program. If we did not have a function called *print_stars()*, we would be forced to write the code to print a line of stars each time we desired this type of output.

2)   Once a function has been written, it may be (re)used in other programs. For example, in our previous lab, we had a function called *print_heading()* which

was used to print out the school heading for the ONE TIME SCHOOL. Now that we have written this function and determined that it prints exactly the way we wish, we may include this function in any program that we write in the future for this school. **This code will never have to be written again!**

3)   Using functions properly will allow us to formulate a program solution that consists of totally independent units. In the "real" world, most large, complex programs are not actually written by one individual, but are the result of a team of programmers. Each team member will be responsible for certain portions of the program. After a period of time, these portions are combined to create the final project. Since team work of this fashion is common, it is necessary for each team member to write separate, independent functions.

4)   Remember that functions should have one specific purpose to aid in the top-down design process. When it becomes necessary to debug a program, it is much easier to debug each individual function rather than to attempt to debug the long, complicated algorithms that may be involved in the program.

B.   C++ Common Library Functions

There are many useful functions that have been previously written and are available in C++ libraries. To be able to use these functions, it is necessary for us to:

1)   become familiar with various available functions.
2)   learn how to gain access to these functions.
3)   learn to use supplied functions when they are needed in a program.

In C++, these available functions are grouped together into libraries according to their purpose. These libraries are collections of object modules (functions) which will be loaded at link time if a function is requested.   One library which is commonly used is the **math library** which is made available by including the *math.h* header file in the C++ program. This header file, which is similar to the *iostream.h* header file, is a collection of function prototypes and declarations for functions in the math library. The math library includes many mathematical functions including the trigonometric functions, the logarithmic functions and the square root function. Other header files which we have seen previously are *iostream.h* which contains information needed for input/output, and *iomanip.h* which contains various information including setw() and setprecision(). The header file, *time.h*, contains information used in date and time applications.

We now consider functions from the math library and incorporate some of these functions in a program. Here is a sample listing of several mathematical functions found in the math library:

<table>
<tr><td>**Type of Functions**</td><td>**Examples**</td></tr>
</table>

Type of Functions	Examples
trigonometric functions:	$\sin(x)$, $\cos(x)$, $\tan(x)$, acos (x), asin(x) and atan(x).
conversion functions:	ceil (x) = smallest integer not less than x.

ceil $(2.95)=3$
ceil $(3.01)=4$

floor $(x)=$ largest integer not greater than x.

floor $(2.95) = 2$
floor $(3.01) = 3$

fabs (x) = absolute value of x

arithmetic functions:	sqrt (x) = square root of x
	pow $(x,y) = x^y$

NOTE: In each of the above examples, x and y are of floating-point type and all functions return a value of the same type except for the *ceil* and *floor* conversion functions. The arguments for the square root must be non-negative. In addition, arguments for *cos*, *sin* and *tan* must be expressed in radians. The functions *acos*, *asin* and *atan* return a value expressed in radians.

EXERCISE 1:   Evaluate the following C++ expressions which use functions included in the math library. Show all answers on the provided answer sheet. If invalid, so indicate.

1) ceil(25.899)   2) floor (-25.01)   3) sqrt(-4.0)
4) ceil(-42.55)   5) sqrt (sqrt(16.0))   6) floor (4.0)

To use a library function in your program, this function must be declared. This is easily accomplished by inserting the following #include directive at the beginning of the program:

#include <name of header file>

#include statements usually appear at the beginning of your source file. If we wish to use the square root function, for example, we would need the following directive:

#include <math.h>

You may wish to use math functions as well as input/output functions, etc. In this case, a program may have several #include statements.

EXERCISE 2:   Suppose that we have been asked to write a program which will input data related to the real solutions to a quadratic equation, output the solutions and the time of day the solutions were printed. Show all #include statements appropriate for this program.

Lastly we must learn how to incorporate these functions when needed. Most library functions can be used anywhere an expression is indicated. Consider the following unrelated examples:

   a)   answer = acos(x) + asin(x);
   b)   cout << fabs(answer);
   c)   height = ceil(x);
   d)   cout << "The square root of" << x << "is" << sqrt (x);

EXERCISE 3:   Translate the following to C++. Use math library functions where necessary.

   1) $X = \dfrac{-b + \sqrt{b^2 - 4ac}}{2a}$

   2)   change y to the largest integer not greater than x.

   3)   print the value of $x(a - 2x)^4$

C.   User-Defined Functions with Input Arguments

Library functions should be used whenever possible since they have (usually) been debugged and tested. However, it is relatively easy to envision the need for functions that are not on the list of library functions provided by C++. We saw in Lab 4 that C++ user functions 1) may or may not have input arguments and 2) may or may not return a single value.

Many functions including library functions require that information be sent to the function so that the function may perform its needed operations. For example, we learned that C++ has a mathematical function called **sqrt (x)**. In order for this function to operate on a number and determine its square root, the function must receive an input value which in this case is called **x**. Therefore, x is called the input argument. Note the arguments in each of the following function call and definition pairs:

function call	function definition header

print_stars(5);   void print_stars (int number)
print_info(old_bal, new_bal);   void print_info (float old, float new)

Both functions (*print_stars* and *print_info*) require input from the calling statement. In *print_stars()*, the number 5 is sent to the function so the function will know exactly how many stars to print. The function *print_info()* needs to receive the old checking account balance and the new checking account balance so that these values can be printed.

There are two types of arguments in a C++ program: formal arguments and actual arguments. Actual arguments are the values or variables listed in the function call. In the examples above, *5, old_bal* and *new_bal* are actual arguments. Formal arguments are the variables included in the function header argument list. Remember that a function header is the first line of the definition of the function. It provides the return type, the name of the function, and a list of formal arguments with types. Thus in the examples above, *number, old* and *new* are formal arguments. Formal arguments **must** be given a type.

STYLE COMMENT!! As we have noted previously, all function definitions should include comments. Make sure you realize where a comment is appropriate in a definition. Always include comments related to the input arguments explaining each argument!

EXERCISE 4: Write a function definition **header** for a function needed to calculate and print the cost of laying carpet in a room, given the size of the room (length and width) and the price of the carpet/square foot. **NOTE:** The function should receive input. Therefore, be sure to use appropriate formal arguments and show appropriate comments for the function header. For example, if a function to find and print the maximum of 3 grades were required, the function header and comments might appear as:

```
//  Function:  maximum
//  Purpose:   This function finds and prints the maximum
//             of three grades

void maximum (int grade1, int grade2, int grade3) // IN:  three test grades
```

D.   Functions with a Return Value

Often a function is needed to compute a single value and this value is returned to the calling program. We say that this particular function has a return value. We will explore functions which return multiple values in a future lab.

RULE: If a function calculates a single value, this value should be returned to the calling function using the **return** statement.

The following function:

```
// Function:   average
// Purpose:    This function finds and returns the average
//             of three floating point grades received as
//             input arguments.

float average (float test1, float test2, float test3)    //IN: three test scores
{
        float aver;              //average of scores

        aver = (test1 + test2 + test3)/3;
        return (aver);
}
```

is an example of a function which has input arguments and a return value. This function computes the average of the three tests and returns the average using the **return** statement. The word "float" preceding the word "average" in the function header indicates that the value which the function will return will be of type float.

We will now explore functions which receive input arguments and return a single value through the return statement. We will examine two mathematical problems which are related to the quadratic equation. The quadratic equation in mathematics is a function of the form

$$f(x) = ax^2 + bx + c$$

The first problem which we will explore is that of evaluating the function at a specific value for x. The second problem which we will explore is that of finding values of x which make the function have the value 0. In other words we will find the roots of $ax^2 + bx + c = 0$ using the quadratic formula.

EXERCISE 5:   Load the file called **inlab5.cpp** to memory. This program contains a function called *quadratic ()* which receives input arguments for a, b, c, and x and evaluates a quadratic equation which has the form

$$ax^2 + bx + c$$

for a particular value of x. Examine this program and answer the following questions:

   a)   Name the formal arguments for the function *quadratic()*.
   b)   Name the actual arguments.
   b)   What is the return type of this function?

EXERCISE 6:   Compile and execute this C++ program to assure that it solves our first problem of evaluating a quadratic. Try various values for a, b, c and x.

EXERCISE 7: Write a function called *discriminant()* which will compute the value of the discriminant of a quadratic equation. In other words, given the input arguments a, b, and c, this function finds and returns the value of $b^2 - 4ac$. Add this function to the end of the **inlab5.cpp** program.

EXERCISE 8: Add to the main program a function prototype for *discriminant()*. Use the *discriminant* function to calculate the roots of the quadratic equation. Use the following formulas to compute the roots:

$$\text{root1} = \frac{-b + \sqrt{b^2 - 4ac}}{2a}$$

$$\text{root2} = \frac{-b - \sqrt{b^2 - 4ac}}{2a}$$

Add statements to print root1 and root2.

CAUTION: Don't forget to use the **#include <math.h>** directive so that you will have access to the *sqrt()* function.

EXERCISE 9: Compile and test your program on the following test data. Describe the output for each set of data:

a) a = 1, b = 8 and c = 2
b) a = 2, b = 4 and c = 1.5
c) a = -1, b = 2 and c = 4
d) a = 1, b = 2 and c = 4 (Note: This one may give surprising results!! Why?)

EXERCISE 10: Test your program again but leave out the **#include <math.h>** statement. Don't forget to compile before running. Describe what happened.

Lab 5 Files

```
//File:          inlab5.cpp
//Author:
//Purpose:       This program evaluates a quadratic equation of the
//               form:
//                     ax^2 + bx + c
//
//               at a value for x which is input interactively.


//include files...
#include <iostream.h>
#include <iomanip.h>

void main ()
{
    //function prototypes...
    float quadratic (float, float, float, float);       //evaluate a quadratic

    //local variables...
    float a, b, c;                          //coefficients of ax^2 + bx + c
    float value;                            //value at which the quadratic will be evaluated
    float answer;                           //value of the quadratic equation

    //Read in values for a, b, c, and x
    cout << "Please enter coefficients for the quadratic equation";
    cout << endl;
    cin  >> a >> b >> c;
    cout << "Please enter the value at which the quadratic";
    cout << " should be evaluated" << endl;
    cin  >> value;

    //Evaluate the quadratic
    answer = quadratic (a,b,c, value);

    //Display the results
    cout << endl;
    cout << endl;
    cout << "The quadratic equation " << a << "x^2 + ";
    cout << b << "x + " << c << " has a function value of ";
    cout << setprecision (2) << answer << endl;
    cout << "when x = " << value << "." << endl;

    //end of main...
    return;

}



//Function:      quadratic()
//Purpose:       To evaluate and return the quadratic ax^2 + bx + c
//               at a particular value of x
```

```
float quadratic (float a,
                 float b,
                 float c,         //IN: coefficients of the quadratic
                 float x)         //IN: the value of x
{
    //local declarations...
    float answer;                 //the value of the quadratic

    //evaluate and return the value of the quadratic
    answer = a*x*x + b*x + c;
    return answer;
}
```

Lab 5 - Answer Sheet

NAME: _____

EXERCISE 1:

1) _____

2) _____

3) _____

4) _____

5) _____

6) _____

EXERCISE 2:

EXERCISE 3:

1) _____

2) _____

3) _____

EXERCISE 4:

EXERCISE 5:

a)   _____

b)   _____

c)   _____

EXERCISE 9:

a)   _____

b)   _____

c)   _____

d)   _____

EXERCISE 10:

Lab 6

Decision Statements

Objectives:	Learn to use logical expressions
	Learn to use if and if-else statements
	Learn to use the switch statement

In Lab 2, we discovered that the basic building blocks for algorithm development included the sequence, the decision statement, and the loop. Thus far, most of our labs have dealt solely with the sequence construct. However, in Labs 4 and 5 we saw the decision statement in some of our examples. If the decision statement had been used in the last exercises of Lab 5, the input data could have been tested in order to avoid division by zero or taking the square root of a negative number. In this lab, we will explore the C++ decision statement.

A. Logical Expressions

When we solve the problem of finding a person's pay, we might ask the question "Did the person work more than 40 hours?" If so, overtime pay would be paid to this individual. In C++, we can determine if overtime pay is needed by evaluating a logical expression.

A **logical expression** is an expression which has two possible values: 0 if the expression is false and non-zero (often 1) if it is true. A logical expression involves the use of a relational operator and/or a logical operator. A list of these C++ operators and their meaning appear below:

Relational Operators

Operator	Meaning
<	less than
<=	less than or equal to
>	greater than
>=	greater or equal to
==	equal to
!=	not equal to

Logical Operators

&&	and
¦¦	or
!	not

Examples:

	logical expression	meaning
a)	x < 2	Is x less than 2?
b)	b*b - 4*a*c > 0	Is b^2-4ac greater than 0?
c)	answer == 'Y'	Is answer equal to 'Y'?

In the above example, if x = 5, a = 1, b = 4, c = 1, and answer = 'N' then the logical expression a) evaluates to false, b) evaluates to true, and c) evaluates to false.

Note: A common error is to confuse the assignment operator = with the equality operation ==. Care must be used to avoid this mistake as surprising results will occur.

Logical operators are used to form more complicated logical expressions. For example, to determine if a person's age was between 14 and 18, we might say in English "age is greater than or equal to 14 and age is less than or equal to 18". In C++ this would be expressed as:

$$(age >= 14) \ \&\& \ (age <= 18)$$

The parentheses are included for readability only since relational operators are performed before logical operators in C++. One should refer to an operator precedence chart for a complete list of precedence rules. Below is a brief chart showing the order from highest to lowest for a few selected operators:

Highest   !
             *, /,%

```
               +, -
               <, <=, >, >=
               ==, !=
               &&
Lowest         ¦¦
```

The && (and) operator yields a true result only when both of its operands are true and the ¦¦ (or) operator yields a false result only when both of its operands are false. The ! (not) operator yields the opposite truth value of its single operand.

Examples:

(3 < 5) && (5 == 4+1)	truth value is true
(8 == 6*2) && (12 < 15)	truth value is false
(8 == 6*2) ¦¦ (12 < 15)	truth value is true
(8 == 6*2) ¦¦ (12 > 15)	truth value is false
!(3 < 5)	truth value is false

The parentheses are optional in all of the examples above except for the last logical expression. In the last expression, the parentheses are necessary to cause the operator < to be performed before the !.

EXERCISE 1:   Write the following English expressions as C++ expressions:

a) *weight* greater than 100   b) *a* equal to 0
c) *hours* less than or equal to 40   d) *x* is between 10 and 20 inclusive
e) *answer* is 'Y' or 'y'

EXERCISE 2:   Evaluate (tell the truth value for) the following C++ expressions. Assume i=5, j=6, k=8.

a) i+1 >= j
b) j%k < j/i
c) i + (j - 3) == k
d) (i > j) ¦¦ (k > j)
e) i/j == 0
f) !(i > j) && (k > j)

B. The *if* and *if-else* Decision Statements

As mentioned previously, algorithms often make a decision between two activities depending on the outcome of some test. A C++ programmer can represent this process using an if or an if-else statement. Sometimes we wish to test a condition and, if the condition is true, to perform a set of statements. For example, suppose we had written the following design and wished to translate it to C++.

```
pay = rate * hours
if hours > 40 then
    pay = pay + (hours - 40) * .5 * rate
Display the pay
```

In C++, this design becomes:

```
1       pay = rate * hours;
2       if (hours > 40)                 // add overtime pay
3           pay = pay + (hours - 40) * .5 * rate;
4       cout << "Pay = " << pay << endl;
```

Statement #3 will only be executed when the logical expression (hours > 40) is true. Whether the logical expression is true or false, statement #4 is executed. In general, the if has the following form:

```
if (logical expression)
    statement to be executed if true;
```

or

```
if (logical expression)
{
    statement1;
    statement2;
        ...
    statementn;
}
```

The statements between the { and the } are called a block of statements and if the logical expression is true, every statement in the block will be executed. If the expression is false, then none of the statements will be performed. An example of this form follows,

```
1       pay = hours * rate;
2       if (hours > 40)
3       {
4           overtime = (hours - 40)* .5 * rate;
```

```
5        cout << "Overtime pay is: " << overtime << endl;
6        pay = pay + overtime;
7    }
8    cout << "Pay = " << pay << endl;
```

If the hours worked were greater than 40, lines 4, 5 and 6 would be performed.

EXERCISE 3: Write C++ *IF* statements for the following:

a)   If *height* is greater than 5.0 and *weight* is less than 90, print the message "underweight".

b)   If *radius* is greater than zero, calculate the area of the circle and print the results.

EXERCISE 4:

a)   What is the output of the following, assuming x = 5?
```
     if (x >= 6)
             cout << "Was greater" << endl;
     cout << "Who knows" << endl;
```
b)   What is the output if x = 6?

Sometimes we wish to perform one set of statements if a logical expression is true and an alternative set of statements if a logical expression is false. The general form of the C++ if-else statement is:

```
     if (logical expression)
        true-statement;
     else
        false-statement;
```

or

```
     if (logical expression)
        true-statement block;
     else
        false-statement block;
```

Examples:

a)   Express the English statement "If the score is greater than or equal 70, the student is passing; otherwise the student is failing." The solution is:

```
     if (score >= 70)
```

```
            cout << "passing" << endl;
        else
            cout << "failing" << endl;
```

b) Calculate the real roots of the quadratic equation if they exist and print a message otherwise. The solution is:

```
discr = b * b - 4 * a * c;
if (discr >= 0)
{
    root1 = (-b + sqrt(discr))/(2*a);
    root2 = (-b - sqrt(discr))/(2*a);
    cout << "The two roots are: " << endl;
    cout << root1 << endl;
    cout << root2 << endl;
}
else
{
    cout << "The discriminant was negative." << endl;
    cout << "There are no real roots." << endl;
}
```

EXERCISE 5:   Write the following using the C++ *if-else* statement:

a)   If age is less than 21, print a message saying "You can't vote"; otherwise print a message saying "You can vote - Congratulations!"

b)   If classification is equal to 5 then set the character variable *class_type* equal to 'G', and print a message saying "graduate student"; otherwise set *class_type* equal to 'U' and print a message saying "undergraduate".

Sometimes we have multiple alternative decisions instead of two way decisions. When this is true, we can still use the if-else statement. As an example, suppose we wish to determine whether a number, say num, is positive, zero or negative and print an appropriate message. To do this, we can use a nested if. The following C++ code solves this problem.

```
if (num > 0)
    cout << "positive";
else
    if (num == 0)
        cout << "equal zero";
    else
        cout << "negative";
cout << endl;
```

This nested if can be written as a multiway if as follows:

```
if (num < 0)
    cout << "positive";
else if (num == 0)
    cout << "equal zero";
else
    cout << "negative";
cout << endl;
```

EXERCISE 6:   Consider the following multiway if which tells an Olympic participant which medal would be won based on his/her final score in an event. Assume that only the top two medals are of interest.

```
if (score >= 97)
    cout << "Gold";
else if (score >= 94)
    cout << "Silver";
else
    cout << "Try again in four years";
cout << endl;
```

Rewrite the above segment if the participant was also interested in the Bronze medal and could get it with a score greater than or equal 89.

C. Switch Control Statement

The *switch* control statement may also be used in C++ to select one of several alternatives. The *switch* statement has the form:

```
switch (expression)
{
    case 1stvalue:      statement(s)1;
                        break;
    case 2ndvalue:      statement(s)2;
                        break;
        ...
    case nthvalue:      statement(s)n;
                        break;
    default:            statement(s)n+1;
                        break;
}
```

For example:

```
switch (letter_grade)
{
  case 'A':
      cout << "Excellent";
      break;
  case 'B':
      cout << "Good Job";
      break;
  case 'C':
      cout << "Average";
      break;
  case 'F':
      cout << "See you again next year";
      break;
  default:
      cout << "Error in letter grade:" << letter_grade;
      break;
}
cout << endl;
```

Note: The word **break** in a switch is very important! If the break is omitted following a statement sequence, then execution will continue, or fall through to the next statement(s). Sometimes this is desirable, as shown in the example below where multiple cases share the same outcome:

```
switch (size)
{
  case 1:
  case 2:
  case 3:
      cout << "small";
      break;
  case 4:
  case 5:
      cout << "medium";
      break;
  case 6:
      cout << "large";
      break;
  default:
      cout << "error";
      break;
}
```

EXERCISE 7: Rewrite the multiway if for the Olympic participant from Exercise 6 using a switch statement.

EXERCISE 8: Load **inlab6.cpp** to memory. Examine it carefully. Several errors have been made in the if, if-else, and switch statements. Eliminate the errors and turn in a corrected version of the program along with a "clean" compile and a "run". (Some errors are syntax errors - the compiler generates an error or warning to help you find the error. At least one error will cause the output to be incorrect.)

Lab 6 Files

```
//File:          inlab6.cpp
//Author:
//Purpose:       This program calculates grades for a student
//               in Mr. Smith's mathematics class.
//               Several errors have been made in the if statements
//               and switch statements.

//include files...
#include <iostream.h>

void main()
{
    //function prototypes..
    void print_class(int);          //function to print a student's
                                    //classification.

    void pass_or_fail(int tst1,
                      int tst2,
                      int tst3);    //determine pass/fail status

    //local declarations..
    int classification;             //classification of a student
    int tst1, tst2, tst3;           //three test scores

    // input student's information
    cout << "Enter the student's classification (1 = freshman,"
         << endl;
    cout << "2 = sophomore, etc.): ";
    cin  >> classification;


    //check for a valid class and proceed accordingly
    if (classification >= 1 && classification <= 5)

        //display classification
        print_class (classification);

        // get the three test scores
        cout << "Enter three test scores: ";
        cin  >> tst1 >> tst2 >> tst3;

        //find average and display pass/fail status
        pass_or_fail(tst1, tst2, tst3);

    else
        cout << "You entered an invalid class " <<endl;

    //end of main...
    return;
}
```

```
//Function:        Print_class()
//Purpose:         Print whether a student is a freshman, sophomore,
//                 etc.  Sent to this function is an integer, classification,
//                 which indicates which class the student is in..

void print_class(int classification)        //IN: the student's classification
{
    cout << "Your classification is " ;
    switch (classification)
    {
        case 1: cout << "freshman";
        case 2: cout << "sophomore";
        case 3: cout << "junior";
        case 4: cout << "senior";
        case 5: cout << "graduate";
    }
    cout << endl;
    return;
}


//Function:        pass_or_fail()
//Purpose:         This function determines a student's average
//                 based on three test scores.  Finally, the
//                 pass/fail status of the student is determined
//                 and printed.

void pass_or_fail(int tst1,
                  int tst2,
                  int tst3)        //IN:  The student's scores
{
    //local declarations...
    float average;                    //test average
    char next_class;                  //go on to the next class? (y=yes,n=no)

    //calculate the average score
    average = (tst1 + tst2 + tst3)/3.0;

    //determine pass/fail status
    if average >= 70
    {
        cout << "You passed! " << endl;
        next_class = 'Y';
    }
    else
    {
        cout << "You failed! " << endl;
        next_class = 'N';
    }
    if (next_class = 'Y')      //Be careful on this line!
        cout << "Good luck in the next class!"<< endl;
    return;
}
```

Lab 6 - Answer Sheet

NAME: _____

EXERCISE 1:

a) _____

b) _____

c) _____

d) _____

e) _____

EXERCISE 2:

a) _____   b) _____

c) _____   d) _____

e) _____   f) _____

EXERCISE 3:

a)

b)

EXERCISE 4:

      a)   _____

               _____

      b)   _____

               _____

EXERCISE 5:

      a)

      b)

EXERCISE 6:

EXERCISE 7:

Lab 7

Looping Constructs

Objectives:	To learn the looping constructs provided in C++ To learn the C++ syntax for each looping construct To provide experience in using loops

One of the basic building blocks of an algorithm is the loop structure. In this lab we will discuss the different types of looping constructs which are available in C++. First, consider the following:

1.   A **looping construct** is a structure provided by a language which allows a block of statements to be executed repeatedly.

2.   There are basically two kinds of loops:

   a) controlled loops (those that terminate)
   b) uncontrolled loops (those that do not terminate)

   However, **only** controlled loops should be used in programming. To prepare ourselves for the unexpected, we will study both types of loops in this lab.

3.   A **controlled loop** contains some repetition condition which will eventually force the looping construct to terminate. We call this the exit condition.

4.   An uncontrolled loop may never stop so we call this type of loop an infinite loop. In other words, an infinite loop either contains no exit condition to allow the loop to terminate or the exit condition for the loop is never met.

5. A controlled loop contains a test for exit conditions. This "test" for exit must be placed appropriately within the looping construct.

6. Some loops have a special variable called a **counter** which counts specific items or values and causes the execution of the loop to terminate when the counter has incremented or decremented a set number of times. We call this type of loop a **counting loop** (or definite loop).

C++, as well as many other languages, provides three looping constructs: the *while*, the *do-while* and the *for* loop. First, we will study the characteristics of each of these loops and then show the syntax for each looping structure.

A.   The C++ *WHILE* Loop

The <u>*WHILE*</u> looping construct:

1. contains the condition and test for exit at the beginning of the loop. Since the exit condition and test appear before the first instruction in the loop, the *WHILE* looping construct is called a *pre-test* loop.

2. gives no guarantee that the loop will even execute since the exit condition is evaluated at the beginning of the loop.

3. executes all statements in the loop while a conditional statement is true.

4. usually requires previous statements prior to the *WHILE* to initialize the variables in the loop exit condition. This is necessary since the exit condition is tested at the beginning of the loop.

The syntax for a *while* loop is:

A) *while* (logical expression)
       statement;

       or

B) *while* (logical expression)
       block;

Note that there are two forms for the *while* loop. Form A is used if there is only one statement to be placed in the loop. Form B should be used if more than one statement is to be placed in the loop. A **block**, as discussed in Lab 6, is a group of statements surrounded by the opening brace, {, and closing brace ,}. Note also that the statement or block is executed **after** the logical expression is evaluated.

Since the exit condition in a *while* loop is tested before any of the statements in the loop, any variables appearing in the logical expression **must** receive values before the *while* is entered. Thus, the variables may be initialized using an assignment statement prior to the *while*.

Alternately, a *while* loop may require a PRIME READ - an input statement that appears BEFORE the *while* loop is entered. The example below demonstrates a prime read:

```
10      cin >> x;
11      while ( x < 10)
12      {
13              cout << x << endl;
14              cin >> x;
15      }
```

We say that line 10 "primes" the *while* loop. The variable *x* must have a value before the *while* condition can be evaluated. Line 11 denotes the exit condition (x < 10). This means this loop will continue to print the value of *x* as long as *x* is < 10.

EXERCISE 1:   Write a C++ program segment which will read in two integers (hours and rate) and then compute and print the pay. Continue performing this process until the user types in a negative number for the hours. Use a *while* loop with a prime read.

EXERCISE 2:   The following are *WHILE* loop applications. Write C++ *while* logical expressions to represent the exit condition for each application. Also, decide how to initialize each loop.

   a.   Read in values for x and print them while x is positive.
   b.   Continue to get and process data as long as the user wishes to continue this process. The user will enter the character 'y' indicating that he wishes to continue this process. If another character is entered, the process should terminate.

B.   The C++ *DO-WHILE* Loop

The <u>*DO-WHILE*</u> looping construct:

   1.   contains the condition and test for exit at the end of the loop. We call this

a *post-test* loop since the exit condition occurs after the last instruction in the loop and the loop statements are executed **before** the test is performed.

2. guarantees that the loop will always execute at least one time.

3. executes all the statements in the loop while a condition is true.

As an example of a situation which might use the *do-while* loop, suppose we wish to read and process employee information until the last employee is processed. And suppose that we have determined that the last employee has an ID of 999. Thus, the C++ expression to represent the exit condition for the loop would be **ID != 999**.

The syntax for the *do-while* loop is:

A) *do*
    statement1;
    while (logical expression);
or

B) *do*
    block;
    while (logical expression);

Note again that Form B should be used if more than one statement is to be placed in the loop and that a block is a group of statements surrounded by opening and closing braces. (In a *do-while* loop, the statement or block is executed first and then the logical expression is evaluated.)

If we wish to process employees until the last employee is processed and we know that the last employee has an ID of 999, then the following *do-while* loop might be used.

```
        do
        {
            .
            .
            .
        }
        while (ID != 999);
```

EXERCISE 3:   Write a C++ program segment which will read in values for the variable, *grade*, until *grade* has a value between 0 and 100. Use a *do-while* loop.

EXERCISE 4:   Each of the following problems should use *do-while* loops. Write a

C++ conditional expression (x < 10, for example) to represent the exit condition in each case.

a.   Process and print out the grades for different students until the user indicates that he/she no longer wishes to process grades. The user indicates this by typing in the character 'N' to indicate that he/she no longer wishes to process information.

b.   Continue to read in values for A, B, and C until a positive discriminant (B^2 - 4AC) is found.

C.   The *FOR* Loop

The *FOR* looping construct:

1.   contains a counter which is:

    a)   initialized (given a starting value)
    b)   tested against a final value for the exit condition
    c)   incremented or decremented (the counter is updated before the next test for exit)

2.   gives no guarantee that the loop will ever be executed since the exit condition is evaluated at the beginning of the loop. Therefore, the *for* looping construct is also called a *pre-test* loop.

The *for* loop causes a set of instructions to be repeated while some counter lies within a range of values. For example, if we wished to calculate the pay for exactly 10 employees, a *for* loop would be appropriate. In this case, the counter would take on the values 1, 2, 3,...,10 during processing.

The syntax of the *for* loop is:.

A)   *for* (initialize counter; test counter; update counter)
        statement;

or

B)   *for* (initialize counter; test counter; update counter)
        block;

Consider the following "*for* loop" examples:

EXAMPLE 1:

```
for (int i=1; i < 11; i++)
        cout << i << endl;
```

This loop structure will execute exactly 10 times and will print out the integers from 1 to 10. Each integer will appear on a separate line.

Note that:

1)   *i* is the loop control variable.
2)   *i* begins with the value 1.
3)   *i* is incremented (increased by 1) **after** the loop is executed.
4)   This loop terminates when *i* has a value that is no longer less than 11. Therefore, the loop will terminate when *i* has the value 11.
5)   The scope of the variable *i* in this example is limited to the *for* loop since *i* is declared in the *for* statement. This means that the variable *i* is visible (can be used) **only** in the *for* loop.
6)   All loop control variables should be declared a) in the function in which the loop appears or b) in the *for* loop itself as in the above example.
7)   The variable *i* in the above example will be undefined after the loop termination since it was declared in the *for* loop itself.

EXAMPLE 2:

```
for (int j=2; j< 5; j++)
{
        cin >> x;
        cout<< x << endl;
}
```

This loop will read in and print out exactly 3 values for x. A value will be read when *j* is 2, when *j* is 3 and when *j* is 4. Each value will be printed on a separate line.

Note that:

1)   *j* is the loop control variable in this example.
2)   *j* begins with the value 2.
3)   This loop terminates when *j* is no longer less than 5. Thus, this loop will terminate when *j* is equal to 5.

4)   This is an example of a loop which contains a block in the body of the loop.

5)   *j*'s scope is limited to the *for* loop and *j* is undefined after the loop termination.

EXAMPLE 3:

```
for (int j=10; j>0; j--)
        cout << endl;
```

This loop will print out 10 blank lines.

Note that:

1)   *j* is the counter in this example.
2)   *j* begins with the value 10.
3)   *j* is decreased by 1 each time through the loop.
4)   This loop terminates when *j* is equal to 0.
5)   *j* is an int whose scope is the loop. It is undefined after the loop terminates.

EXAMPLE 4:

```
for (int j=10; j>0; j--);
        cout << "HELLO";
```

This loop is tricky!! It will count 10 times and then will print out the word "HELLO" one time! **WHY?** --a semicolon is inappropriately placed after the for statement!!

EXERCISE 5:   Fill in the blanks related to the following C++ program segment. Show all answers on the provided answer sheet!

```
for (int k=-5; k<0; k++)
        cout<< k + 2 << endl;
        cout<<"HELLO";
```

1)   _____ is the counter in this example.
2)   The counter begins with the value _____.
3)   The counter is _____ (increased or decreased) by _____ each time through the loop.
4)   This loop terminates when the counter reaches the value _____.
5)   Show exact output for this program segment. BE CAREFUL!! IT'S A TRICKY QUESTION!

EXERCISE 6:   Each of the following are *for* loop applications. Show the beginning value, the test value and the update method for the counter in each question. NOTE: Answers should appear similar to: (j=1; j<11; j++)

    a)   Find and print out the area for five triangles.

    b)   Compute the average for each of N students, where N is the number of students.

Styling note: Whatever loop construct is used, the statements inside the loop should be indented for clarity.

D.   Three C++ Looping Constructs

In summary, C++ provides three looping constructs each of which has its own particular purpose and specifications.

EXERCISE 7:   Explain whether the following characteristics apply to the *while* loop (W), the *do while* loop (D), the *for* loop (F), ALL of the looping constructs (A), NONE of the looping constructs (N), or a combination of looping constructs. If a characteristic applies to several looping constructs, list all constructs for which the characteristic applies.

    a)   An exit condition is used to exit the loop.
    b)   Is repeated a fixed number of times.
    c)   The statements contained in the loop may never be executed.
    d)   Is always executed at least one time.
    e)   Is called a post-test loop.
    f)   Is called a pre-test loop.
    g)   Contains a counter.
    h)   Could possibly be an infinite loop.
    i)   Exit condition appears at beginning of loop.
    j)   Contains an exit condition in the middle of the loop.
    k)   Exits the loop when a condition is false.
    l)   Exits the loop when a condition is true.

Now that you are familiar with the different kinds of loops and their characteristics, make sure that you can distinguish between each type and when each type should be used. A programmer should ask the following questions when writing a program:

    1)   If a loop is needed, what should be placed inside the loop? (i.e. what statements should be repeated?)

2)   If a loop is needed, what is the exit condition?

3)   What type of loop should be used and why? The following may aid in answering this question!

If it is known beforehand exactly how many times the loop should execute, choose a *for* loop.

Does the loop need to execute at least one time? If the answer is yes, use a *do-while* loop.

Is it possible that the statements in the loop should not execute at all? If the answer is yes, use a *while* loop.

Consider the following example and analysis:

Example: We wish to write a program which will play a guessing game called "GUESS A NUMBER" with the computer. The program will randomly pick a number between one and fifty and the user will try to guess the number. The computer will then give clues depending on whether the number guessed by the user was too low or too high. The computer will count the number of guesses by the user and print out the number of guesses at the end of the game.

1)   <u>What should we put inside the loop?</u>   After the computer "thinks" of a number, the following instructions should be placed in the loop:

1.   Let the user guess a number
2.   Increment (add one to) the count for the number of guesses
3.   Tell the user that his guess is too high, too low or JUST right!

2)   <u>What is the exit condition?</u> The correct number is guessed by the user.

3)   <u>What type of loop should be used?</u> *Do-while* loop

4)   <u>Why was this particular looping construct chosen?</u> It is not known beforehand exactly how many times the loop should execute since we do not know how many times the user will guess before he guesses the right number. This rules out a FOR loop. We know that the loop does need to execute at least one time - this is a guessing game so the user MUST guess at least one number. Therefore, we know that a *do-while* loop should be used for this problem.

EXERCISE 8:   Look at each of the following problems and **answer the above questions** for each. DO NOT WRITE CODE!

a)   Ask the user to type in an integer and print out the number of digits in the number. HINT: In order to print out the number of digits in the number, the computer should continue to read in digits one at a time and count them until a carriage return is read.

b)   Continue to read and print integers as long as the integer is not negative. (DO NOT PRINT THE INTEGER IF IT IS NEGATIVE.)

c)   You have 30 employees in your company and you wish to write a note to each one of them and inform them of their new salary increases. It is necessary to read in an employee's name and salary increase and print a letter for each.

E. Finding Syntax Errors

Lastly, common errors encountered when using looping structures will be studied. Consider the following loop example:

```
x=200;
while (x > 100)
   cout << x << endl;
   x= x - 10;
```

Do you see the fatal mistake in this program segment? The above example contains an infinite loop! This loop will continue to print the value "200" forever because the value for *x* is never changed. The programmer used improper syntax for a *while* loop.   Two statements should have been places in the loop. However, the programmer neglected to surround the statements with a { and a }. Therefore, there was only one statement in the loop - *cout << x << endl;*

EXERCISE 9:   Load **inlab7.cpp** to memory. This program is listed below for your convenience. Study the program carefully. It contains four syntax errors and one logic error. Correct these errors and then compile and run the program. HINT: You may wish to compile first to help you find the syntax errors.

```
//File:        inlab7.cpp
//Author:
//Purpose:     This program inputs information about an employee and
//             calculates the employee's pay.  This process is continued
//             until the user indicates that he/she desires to quit.

//NOTE:        This program has exactly four syntax errors
//             and one logic error.  All errors are related to
//             loops.  Read the comments carefully for each
```

```
//                  function to determine the purpose of each one.

//include files...
#include <iostream.h>
#include <iomanip.h>

void main ()
{
    //function prototypes...
    void asterisks (int);           //print asterisks
    int get_hrs ();                 //get hours worked
    float get_rate ();              //get rate of pay
    void print_pay (float, int,
                    float, int);    //print pay
    char prompt_for_more ();        //get more?

    //local declarations...
    char answer;                    //answer determines whether to
                                    //repeat the process
    float rate_of_pay;              //rate of pay per hour
    int hours_worked;               //hours worked
    int id_number;                  //ID of the employee
    float over_time_pay;            //employee overtime
    float pay_amount;               //employee pay

    //process employees while the user says there are more
    do
    {
            asterisks (30);

            // get the employee's data
            hours_worked = get_hrs ();
            rate_of_pay = get_rate ();
            cout << "Please enter your id number" << endl;
            cin  >> id_number;

            //calculate the pay
            if (hours_worked <= 40)
                pay_amount = rate_of_pay * hours_worked;
            else
            {
                over_time_pay = (hours_worked - 40) * rate_of_pay * 1.5;
                pay_amount = 40 * rate_of_pay + over_time_pay;
            }
            print_pay (rate_of_pay, hours_worked, pay_amount, id_number);
            answer = prompt_for_more();
    }
    while answer =='y';

    //end of main...
    return;
}
```

```
//Function:        Asterisks
//Purpose:         This function prints a line of asterisks.

void asterisks (int howmany)        //IN:  how many asterisks to print
{
    for (i=0; i<howmany; i++)
        cout << "*";
    cout << endl;
    return;
}


//Function:        get_hrs
//Purpose:         This function reads (and returns) the number of hours
//                 an employee worked.  Only positive values are
//                 accepted for the hours worked.

//                 BE CAREFUL WITH THIS ONE!!  Is this function doing
//                 what this description says it should?

int get_hrs ()
{
    //local declarations...
    int hours;                      // the number of hours worked

    // get the number of hours worked
    do
    {
        cout << "Please enter the hours worked" << endl;
        cin  >> hours;
    }
    while (hours > 0);
    return hours;
}


//Function:        get_rate()
//Purpose:         This function reads in the rate of pay of an employee
//                 Only positive values are accepted for the rate.

//                 Is this function doing what this description says it should?

float get_rate ()
{
    //local declarations...
    float rate = -1;                //rate of pay per hour

    //get the rate of pay per hour
    do while (rate < 0)
    {
        cout << "Please enter the pay rate per hour" << endl;
        cin  >> rate;
    }
```

```
        return rate;
}


//Function:       print_pay
//Purpose:        This function prints an employee's pay check.

void print_pay (float hour_rate,        //IN: rate of pay/hour
                int number_hours,       //IN: hours worked
                float pay,              //IN: pay amount
                int id)                 //IN: employee id
{
    asterisks(10);
    asterisks(10);
    setprecision (2);
    cout << "EMPLOYEE #:   " << id << endl;
    cout << "PAY AMOUNT:  $" << pay << endl;
    cout << "RATE OF PAY: $" << hour_rate << endl;
    cout << "HOURS WORKED: " << number_hours << endl;
    return;
}


//Function:       prompt_for_more
//Purpose:        This program asks the user whether
//                to continue or not.  Only a 'y' or 'n'
//                answer is accepted as valid input.  The
//                user's response is returned to the calling
//                program.

char prompt_for_more ()
{
    //local declarations...
    char answer;                            //the user's response

    do
    {
        cout << "Do you wish to continue, y or n?" ;
        cin  >> answer;
        cout << endl;
    }
    while (answer != 'y') && (answer != 'n');
    return answer;
}
```

Lab 7 - Answer Sheet

NAME:_____

EXERCISE 1:

EXERCISE 2:

    a)   **exit condition:**_____

            initialize:_____

    b)   **exit condition:**_____

            initialize:_____

EXERCISE 3:

EXERCISE 4:

    a)   **exit condition:**   _____

    b)   **exit condition:**   _____

EXERCISE 5:

1)   _____

2)   _____

3)   _____

4)   _____

5)

EXERCISE 6:

a)   _____

b)   _____

EXERCISE 7:

a)   _____   b)   _____

c)   _____   d)   _____

e)   _____   f)   _____

g)   _____   h)   _____

i)   _____   j)   _____

k)   _____   l)   _____

EXERCISE 8:

a)   **What should be placed inside the loop?**

What is the exit condition?

What type of loop should be used?

Why was this particular looping construct chosen?

b) What should be placed inside the loop?

What is the exit condition?

What type of loop should be used?

Why was this particular looping construct chosen?

c) What should be placed inside the loop?

What is the exit condition?

What type of loop should be used?

Why was this particular looping construct chosen?

Lab 8

Debugging and Testing

Objectives:	Review different types of errors
	Learn debugging techniques
	Learn testing techniques

A. Types of Errors

Locating errors in a program which we did not write can be very difficult. Even if we write the program ourselves, we may still find it difficult to locate our errors. In this section, the three most common types of errors will be reviewed: **syntax errors, run-time errors,** and **logical errors.**

Typically, you define a problem, then design and implement the solution in C++. You type in your program using the editor and compile it. At this point, you may encounter the dreaded syntax error. A <u>syntax error</u> is an error in the misuse of the language. Syntax errors occur because part of the source program violates one or more of the syntax rules of the language. The compiler issues a <u>syntax error message(s)</u> when an attempt is made to compile a source-code program with a syntax error(s) in it. For example, when you try to compile a program with the following statements, you might see the syntax error message below.

        18   cout << "This statement needs a semicolon"
        19   cout << endl;

*Error lab8exmp.cpp 19 : Statement missing ;

The best way to find and eliminate syntax errors is to be very familiar with the syntax rules of the language. When in doubt, look up the correct structure in the text. When the compiler issues a syntax error message, it always indicates a line number at which the error was found. In the code above, the compiler identified an error on line 19. This line may or may not be the real cause of the error. You should examine lines of code before and after the line identified by the compiler. We can see that the error above actually occurs on line 18 since this statement is not terminated by a semicolon. DO NOT change a statement until you have identified the source of the error message! As you solve more and more problems using C++, the error messages will have more meaning for you.

EXERCISE 1:
   a) Define syntax error.
   b) Give an example of a syntax error (other than leaving off a semicolon).

Eventually (after all syntax errors have been removed), the source code can be compiled with no errors. Isn't this great news? Yes, hallelujah!!! But now the program does not execute properly. Maybe it "aborts" ("bombs", "crashes"). This type of error is known as a run-time error. A **run-time error** occurs during a program run when an event makes further processing impossible. For example, if the following statement were included in a C++ program and the run-time error message below were generated, you should immediately suspect that the variable z must have the value zero.

    12   x = y / z;

Divide error

It is also possible to write a program that has no syntax errors and no run-time errors. Thus it appears to run successfully but to your dismay, it produces incorrect results or tries to run forever. This type of error is called a **semantic error**, or **logical error**, because the computer carried out an action that led to an incorrect final result. A semantic error may or may not lead to a program crash depending upon the nature of the error.

EXERCISE 2:   Both of the following segments of code have either logic errors or run-time errors. Assume that all variables have been declared and assume that each section of code is completely self-contained. For each segment, answer the following questions and show corrected code.

   1) Will it crash?

   2) Does it contain a logical error which produces wrong results?

   3) Does it contain an infinite loop?

a)   //Print even numbers from 2 to 20
```
J=0;
do
{
      J += 2;
      cout << j << endl;
}
while (J != 21);
```

b)   cout<< "What is the customer's code and the cost of the item purchased?\n";
```
cin >>cust_code >>cost;
//give a preferred customer (i.e. a customer code of 1) a 10% discount
if (cust_code = 1)
      cost = .9 * cost;
```

B. Debugging Techniques

When a program has errors (**bugs**) in it, they must be found and corrected. We say, then, that the program must be **debugged**. When you debug a program, you must *first find the error* and then, and only then, should you change the offending source code. It is very unwise to change code in the hope that the error will somehow be caught and simply "go away." Before you fix any errors in your code, you should know the basic cause of the error so that you can fix it properly. The only thing you should try is running the program with different input data to determine the pattern of the unexpected behavior. If there are multiple errors, correct the first error and often other error messages will disappear.

A good rule of thumb is that if the bug isn't immediately obvious, leave the computer and quietly look over a printed copy of the program. Studies show that people who do all of their debugging away from the computer actually get their programs working in less time and in the end, produce better programs than those who continue to work at the machine. Students who debug while sitting in front of a terminal tend to use trial and error to correct their program rather than really attempting to find the bug or bugs. Below, you will find some tips to help you in debugging your programs.

Debugging Rule Number 1: *Always use good software engineering principles in creating a program.* It is much easier to find bugs in a program which uses good software engineering techniques. **Software engineering** is the process of developing and maintaining very large software systems. These techniques include using descriptive variable names, proper indentation, documentation, modularity, etc. For example, it is very hard to find errors in the following program because it is poorly written and does not use proper software engineering techniques.

//This program finds the area of a circle after the radius is entered. The formula used is
//pi * radius squared.
#include <iostream.h> void main (){ const float x=3.14159;
float y,z; int n,w ; cout <<"Hello, this program finds and displays the area of a circle"<<
endl;
cout <<"Enter the radius" ; cin >>y; z=x*y*y;
cout << "The area of the circle is" << z <<endl;}

EXERCISE 3:   On the answer sheet, rewrite the program above using proper
indentation and descriptive identifiers.

Debugging Rule Number 2: *To help pinpoint errors, use print statements placed at strategic places in the code.* These "print" statements allow us to observe the path of execution and to track the value of certain variables as the program runs. For example, if an answer produced by the program is wrong, we look at the variables used to calculate this answer.
We may output the value of a variable at different places to see where it becomes incorrect.
Once we locate and correct the problem, the print statements are no longer needed in the
code and they can be removed with the editor. Then the program can be recompiled. The
danger is that another error may cause you to need the print statements again after they are
removed. To avoid this problem, C and C++ provide compiler directives *#define, #ifdef*
and *#endif* that allow blocks of statements to physically remain in the source code but,
based on the value of a flag, be included or omitted by the compiler.

Consider the following program:

```
// File:        inlab8a.cpp
// Author:
// Purpose:     Find the maximum of a set of input values.

//include files...
#include <iostream.h>

//#define DEBUG

void main ()
{
    //function prototypes...
    float max();        //function to find the maximum

    //local declarations...
    float largest;      //the largest input value

    //find and display the largest input value
    largest = max();
    cout << "The largest value was "<< largest<<endl;

    //end of main...
```

```
        return;
}

//Function:      max()
//Purpose:       Find the largest of a set of input values.

float max()
{
        //local declarations...
        float num;              // input value
        int count;              // number of input values processed so far
        int howmany;            // how many input values to process
        float tempmax;          // the maximum so far

        // Input how many input values
        cout << "Enter howmany real values you have ";
        cin  >> howmany;

        if (howmany > 0)
        {
                // Initialize the counter and maximum
                count = 1;
                cout << "Enter your real numbers, one per line:"<< endl;
                cin >> tempmax;

                //Determine the maximum
                while (count < howmany)
                {
                        cin >> num;;
                        count++;
                        if (num > tempmax)
                                tempmax = num;
                }
        }
        else
                tempmax = 0;

        return tempmax;
}
```

Debugging prints can be inserted to check the operation of the *while* loop and help to verify its correctness. These prints can be surrounded by the lines:

```
        #ifdef DEBUG
        .
        .
        .
        #endif
```

For example, in the function *max()*, before the *while*, we might insert:

```
        count = 1;
        cin >> tempmax;
        #ifdef DEBUG
           cout << "Initially, Count = "<< count << endl;
           cout << "We will process "<< howmany << " numbers" << endl;
           cout << "The first number processed was "<< tempmax  << endl;
        #endif
        while (count < howmany)
```

In the loop, we might insert prints as follows:

```
        while (count < howmany)
        {
            cin >> num;
            #ifdef DEBUG
               cout << "We have read " << count << " numbers so far.";
               cout  << endl;
               cout << "The last number read was "<< num <<endl;
            #endif
            count++;
            if (num > tempmax)
               tempmax = num;
            #ifdef DEBUG
               cout <<"The maximum so far is :"<< tempmax << endl;
            #endif
        }
        #ifdef DEBUG
            cout << "Finally, count is "<< count <<endl;
            cout << "The maximum is "<< tempmax << endl;
        #endif
        return tempmax;
```

When we want the debugging print statements included in the compiled code, we "un-comment" the *#define DEBUG* line telling the compiler to define a symbol called DEBUG which is used to decide if the print statements are included. Of course, each time we change our mind about the *#define DEBUG* statement, we must recompile; but at least we never have to remove or reenter the debugging statements. It is good practice to use debugging print statements to indicate when a function is called and if it is executing properly. The values in the actual parameters should be printed immediately before and immediately after the call to a function.

EXERCISE 4:   The file **inlab8b.cpp** contains a program to sum N input values. Insert appropriate print statements to verify the correctness of this program. Turn in a listing, compile and, if possible, a test run of the program after you have added debugging prints. A printed copy of this file follows for your convenience.

```
//File:        inlab8b.cpp
//Author:
//Purpose:     Calculate the sum of N values which are to be input.
```

```
//              where N is an input value.
//include files...
#include <iomanip.h>          // header file needed for i/o manipulation
#include <iostream.h>         // header file needed for i/o, cin, cout
#include <stdlib.h>           // standard library

//Function:     get_how_many()
//Purpose:      Read and return a non-negative integer

int get_how_many()
{
    //local declarations...
    int num;                      //the value read

    // read a nonnegative value
    do
    {
        cout << "How many values would you like for me to input?";
        cin >> num;
    }
    while (num < 0);
    cout << endl;

    return num;
}


//Function:     sum_up_values()
//Purpose:      Returns the sum of N input values

int sum_up_values(int howmany)   //IN:  The number of values to sum
{
    //local declarations...
    int i = 0;                    //current integer being summed
    int sum = 0;                  //sum of input values
    int value;                    //an input value

    // Calculate sum of integers
    while (i < howmany)
    {
        cout << "Please enter the next value: ";
        cin >> value;
        cout << endl;
        i++;
        sum += value;
    }
    return(sum);
}

//Note that with main() physically positioned after the functions
//it calls, function prototypes are unnecessary.

void main()
```

```
{
    //local declarations...
    int n;                      // Number of values
    int total;                  //sum of integers

    //read in how many values to sum up
    n = get_how_many();
    total = sum_up_values (n);

    //display the resulting sum
    cout << "The sum of the " << n << " input values is: " << total << endl;

    //end of main...
    return;
}
```

Debugging Rule #3. *Choose sufficient sets of test data* to ensure that every possible path in a program is executed at least once, if possible. Also, be selective in choosing appropriate test data. If you test a function or program by simply using *many* data sets haphazardly, you are not testing "smart". Suppose, for example, you have a program to solve the following problem: Write a program that reads in three integer values and outputs them in order from lowest to highest. Suppose you wish to test your program and you try these three sets of data:

        100, 30, 110
         50, 40, 60
         70, 20, 90

The sets will all return correct results for the following incorrect code (assume swap interchanges two values):

```
    if (first > second)
            swap( first, second);
    else if (first > third)
            swap( first, third);
    else if (second > third)
            swap( second, third);
```

What is wrong with this data? For starters, not enough different possibilities were tried. All three sets represent the same preconditions, (first is greater than second but less than third). For three distinct input values, six different sets of values must be used in order to test all possibilities for this code. Thus, the following data would be sufficient:

        1   2   3
        2   1   3
        3   1   2

```
3     2     1
1     3     2
2     3     1
```

To fully test this problem, we would also include data sets where two or more of the values were equal.

EXERCISE 5:   **Show** test data which should be used to completely test the following segment of code:

```
if (age < 65)
        if (age < 18)
                if (age < 14)
                        cout << "You're too young to work." << endl;
                else
                        cout << "You're too young to vote." << endl;
        else
                cout << "You're too young to retire." << endl;
else
        cout << "Enjoy your golden years." << endl;
```

Debugging Rule #4. *Test modules individually*. One of the advantages of a modular design is that you can test the design long before the code has been written for all modules. If we test each module individually, then we can assemble the modules into a complete program with a much greater confidence in the correctness of the program.

How can we do this? When a module contains calls to other modules which haven't been written yet, we can write a dummy function called a **stub** to satisfy those calls. A stub may take different forms. Note the following:

   a)   A stub may consists of only a "cout" statement that prints a message like "Function xxxxx just got called." The stub is a dummy, but it allows us to determine whether the function is called at the right time by the program or calling function.

   b)   A stub can also be used to print the set of values that are passed to it; this tells us whether or not the module under test is supplying the proper information.

   c)   Sometimes the stub will assign new values to its output parameters to simulate data being read or results being computed to give the module something to keep working on. Since we can choose the values that are returned by the stub, we have better control over the conditions of the test run. The function stub may also need to return a value.

If you are having trouble debugging a particular function, you may want to test it in complete isolation. In that case, you would substitute stubs for all of the functions that it calls. In addition, you would replace the program or function that calls the function with a dummy program, called a **driver.** A **driver** is a program segment which contains the minimum definitions required to call the function being tested. By surrounding a function with a driver and stubs, you gain complete control of the conditions under which it executes. This allows you to try out different situations and combinations until a pattern that pinpoints the bug emerges.

Suppose that we wish to write a program which plays a guessing game between a person and the computer. The computer is to "think" of a random number between 1 and 100 and the person should guess the number (with help from the computer) until the correct answer is chosen. A function to play the game follows:

```cpp
void guess_a_num()
{
    int random_num;        //A random number between 1 and 100
    int guess;             //The number guessed

    random_num = get_random(1,100);
    cout << "Guess a number between 1 and 100";
    cin >> guess;

    while (guess != random_num)
    {
        if (guess > random_num)
        {
            cout << "Your guess was too high, please guess again";
            cin >> guess;
        }
        else if (guess < random_num)
        {
            cout << "Your guess was too low, please guess again\n";
            cin >> guess;
        }
    }

    cout << "Congratulations, you guessed the correct number!!!";
    cout << endl;
}
```

Now we wish to test this function. However, the first line of the function calls the function *get_random()* to obtain a random number. To test the function *guess_a_num()*, we should use a stub for the *get_random()* function:

```cpp
int get_random (int first, int last)
{
    cout << "The function get_random is a stub" << endl;
    cout << "First and Last are " << first << last;
    cout << "It returns a 60" << endl;
```

```
    return 60;
}
```

Using the stub instead of a full-fledged random number generator allows us to test our guessing game for values that we have control over. The line *return 60* could be modified for other "guesses" that the computer might make before the actual random number generator is used.

EXERCISE 6:   Test the following main program by including stubs for each of the indicated functions. The purpose of the program is to input a value representing the radius of a sphere and to calculate and display the area and volume of the sphere. Write stubs that would allow us to test to see if our functions were being called correctly and if arguments were being sent and received correctly. *Note: Do not write the functions used. Write stubs only*. This main program is stored in **inlab8c.cpp**. Modify it to contain stubs for each function. Turn in a listing of the revised program. Also, submit a hardcopy of the run of the program if this is possible on your system.

```
//File:          inlab8c.cpp
//Author:
//Purpose:       The user inputs the radius of a sphere.  The program
//               calculates and displays the volume and area of the
//               sphere.

//include files...
#include <iostream.h>

void main()
{
    //function prototypes...
    float area_sphere (float);          //find area of sphere
    float vol_sphere (float);           //find volume of sphere
    void display_results (float, float, float); //display area & volume

    //variable declarations...
    float radius;                       //the radius of the sphere
    float volume;                       //the volume of the sphere
    float area;                         //the area of the sphere

    //get the radius
    cout << "Please enter the radius of the sphere:";
    cin >> radius;

    //calculate and display the area and volume
    area = area_sphere (radius);
    volume = vol_sphere (radius);
    display_results (radius, area, volume);

    //end of main...
    return;
```

```
}
```

`//******************* Stubs go here ****************************`

Lab 8 - Answer Sheet

NAME: _____

EXERCISE 1:

a) _____

b) _____

EXERCISE 2:

a)   1)   **Will it crash?**_____

       2)   **Does it contain a logical error which produces wrong results?**_____

       3)   **Does it contain an infinite loop?**_____

b)   1)   **Will it crash?**_____

       2)   **Does it contain a logical error which produces wrong results?**_____

       3)   **Does it contain an infinite loop?**_____

EXERCISE 3:

EXERCISE 5:

Lab 9

Function Arguments and Scope

Objective:	Review the use of input arguments in C++
	Introduce functions which return multiple values
	Discuss value and reference arguments
	Explore the scope of identifiers in C++ functions

A.   Introduction

The importance of using top-down design techniques to write a program has been continually noted in previous labs. We learned that using this design technique will result in a "good", modular program which has useful, well-defined functions. In those previous labs, the following topics were covered:

1)   Functions with and without input arguments.

2)   Functions with and without a return value.

3)   Library functions.

4)   Functions with combinations of the above categories. i.e. functions with no return value and with input arguments, functions with a return value and with no input arguments, etc.

In this lab, we will go one step further in the "function discussion" and will present two additional concepts regarding functions which have not been addressed in previous labs:

1) functions which return multiple values. Sometimes it may be necessary, in order to keep function units "modular" and independent, for a function to return **more** than one value to the calling function! You will learn how this is handled in C++.

2) the scope of function variables. Two types of C++ variables will be discussed. These variables are called local variables and global variables. How a variable is "set up" determines the visibility or usefulness of the variable in each function. We say, then, that the programmer must address the "scope" or visibility of all variables used in a C++ program. Therefore, we will look at the scope of variables in a C++ program.

EXERCISE 1: Load the program called **inlab9a.cpp** and answer the following questions. This program is listed below for your convenience.

1) Name all functions with no return value and no input arguments (if any).
2) Name all functions with a return value and no input arguments (if any).
3) Name all functions without a return value and with input arguments (if any).
4) Name all functions with a return value and with input arguments (if any).
5) Name the library functions (if any) used in the program.

```
//Function:      inlab9a.cpp
//Author:
//Purpose:       Updates a checking account given the
//               starting balance and the amount of the
//               check written against the account.

//include files...
#include <iostream.h>
#include <iomanip.h>

//global function protypes...
void print_stars ();

void main ()
{
    //function prototypes...
    void heading ();                          //display bank heading
    void get_data(float&, float&);            //get balance & check amt
    float new_balance (float, float);         //calculate new balance
    char over (float);                        //determine if overdrawn
    void print_info (float, float, float, char);  //display results

    //local declarations...
    float old_balance,                        //starting balance of the account
          check,                              //amount of the check
          balance;                            //new balance
```

```
    char over_drawn;                          //Is the account over drawn? (y-yes, n-no)

    //get the starting balance and check amount
    get_data (old_balance, check);

    //calculate and print the new balance
    heading ();
    balance = new_balance (old_balance,  check) ;
    over_drawn = over (balance);
    print_info (old_balance, check, balance, over_drawn);
    print_stars ();

    //end of main...
    return;
}

//Function:      get_data()
//Purpose:       Input starting checking balance and amount of check.

void get_data (float& old,                    //OUT: starting account balance
               float& amount)                 //OUT: check amount
{

    cout << "Enter balance from previous month" ;
    cout << " and hit <ENTER>" << endl;
    cin  >> old;
    cout << "Enter amount of check and hit <ENTER>" << endl;
    cin  >> amount;
    return;
}

//Function:      heading()
//Purpose:       Print a heading for the bank statement.

void heading ()
{
    cout << endl;
    cout << endl;
    cout << endl;
    print_stars ();
    print_stars ();
    cout <<"*****************FIFTH NATIONAL BANK********************";
    cout << endl;
    cout << "          1515 ONE TIME STREET" << endl;
    cout << "          MANY APPLES, MINNESOTA";
    print_stars ();
    print_stars ();
    return;
}

//Function:      new_balance()
//Purpose:       Compute and return new bank balance.
```

```cpp
float new_balance (float old,                //IN:  starting balance
                   float amount )            //IN:  check amount
{
    return old - amount;
}



//Function:      over()
//Purpose:       Determine if account is overdrawn or not.

char over (float balance)                    //IN:  the new balance

{
    //local declarations...
    char overdrawn;                          //over drawn status

    if (balance < 0)
         overdrawn = 'y';
    else
         overdrawn = 'n';
    return overdrawn;
}



//Function:      print_info()
//Purpose:       Print all banking information.

void print_info (float old,                  //IN:  starting balance
                 float amount,               //IN:  check amount
                 float bal,                  //IN:  ending balance
                 char over)                  //IN:  over drawn indicator
{
    cout << setiosflags (ios::showpoint | ios::fixed);
    cout << endl;
    cout << " OLD BALANCE  CHECK AMOUNT   NEW BALANCE  OVER DRAWN"<<endl;
    cout << endl;
    cout << setprecision (2) << setw (10) << old <<setw (15) << amount;
    cout << setw (15) << bal;
    cout << "        " << over;
    cout << endl;
    return;
}

//Function:      print_stars()
//Purpose:       Print decorative stars.

void print_stars ()
{
    cout << endl;
    cout << "*************************************************************";
    cout << endl;
}
```

B. Functions which Return Multiple Values

In order to keep C++ programs as modular as possible, it soon becomes clear that it may be necessary for some functions to return multiple values to the function which activated (called) them. We say, then, that these functions have **output** arguments and that these arguments are "called by reference." For example, look at the following code. This is a function which "should" obtain data needed in a C++ program (the function header has some missing parameters which will be discussed later):

```
//Function:       get_data ()
//Task:  This program inputs the length and width
//          of a rectangle and returns them to the
//          calling function.

void get_data (_____, _____)
{
        cout << "Please enter the length and width";
        cout << " of the rectangle" << endl;
        cin >> length >> width;
        cout << endl;
        cout << endl;
        return;

}
```

As you can see, this function needs to return exactly two values to the calling function: the length of the rectangle and the width of the rectangle. In our previous labs, a single value was returned via the return statement. In this lab, we must explore the question: **HOW** does C++ return multiple values to the calling program? The answer is simple, it returns multiple values through the argument list in a way very similar to the way it receives multiple input values. First, we will review what we know about input arguments in C++!

Call-by-value arguments

Note the following depiction of a portion of memory before a C++ program is compiled:

```
     address              MEMORY

     1320 ------- >     _____
                       |  _____  |
     1324 -------->    | |_____| |
                       |  _____  |
     1328 -------->    | |_____| |
                       |  _____  |
     1332 -------->    | |_____| |
                       |_____|
     etc
```

Suppose the following declaration occurs in the C++ program:

int one;

At compile time the compiler searches for an available place in memory to store an integer, assigns this memory location the symbolic name of *one*, and reserves this location for an integer. Thus, memory takes on the following new appearance:

MEMORY

address   symbolic name

```
1320  ------->  _____
1324  ------->  _____  <------- one
1328  ------->
etc.
```

The memory location 1324 now has the symbolic name of *one*. After the C++ statement, *one = 1*, is executed, the following picture depicts the new appearance of memory:

MEMORY

address   symbolic name

```
1320  ------->  _____
1324  ------->  ____1_____  <------- one
1328  ------->
etc
```

Suppose that we now wish to call a function and use *one,* as an input argument:

calling statement: answer = dosomething (one);
function heading: int dosomething (int val)

When the function is activated, memory is allocated for another variable called *val* which is totally independent of *one*. The variable *val*, however, will be initialized to the same value that the variable *one* has. ie., *val* will receive the value 1.

MEMORY

address   symbolic name

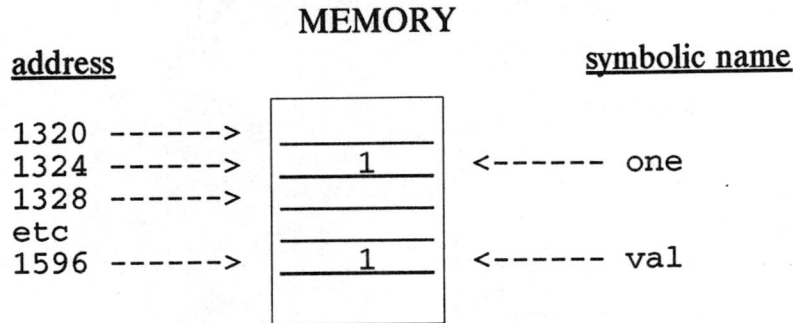

```
1320  ------>  _____
1324  ------>  ____1_____  <------ one
1328  ------>
etc
1596  ------>  ____1_____  <------ val
```

We say that the formal parameter, *val,* is a <u>*call-by-value*</u> parameter since it receives a value from the actual parameter *one.* There is a second type of argument in C++ called a <u>*call-by-reference*</u> argument.

Call-by-reference arguments

Suppose that we have the same situation as before.

MEMORY

<u>address</u>   <u>symbolic name</u>

```
1320  ------>   _____
1324  ------>  |    1    |    <------  one
1328  ------>  |_____|
etc.
```

However, this time we will have the following function call and function heading:

calling statement:	answer = dosomething (one);
function heading:	int dosomething (int& val)

EXERCISE 2:   Describe the difference in **appearance** between this calling/definition pair and the previous calling/definition pair on the preceding page.

In this case the formal parameter called *val* is a <u>*call-by-reference*</u> parameter. This means that the formal parameter *val* is an alias for the actual parameter *one.* This means the two variables *one* and *val* refer to (reference) the same memory address(es). Thus a change to *val* results in a change to *one.*

MEMORY

<u>address</u>   <u>symbolic name</u>

```
1320  ------->   _____
1324  ------->  |    1    |   <------  one, val
1328  ------->  |_____|
etc
```

Therefore, we see that the actual address 1324 in memory has two symbolic names: *one* in the calling function and *val* in the *dosomething()* function. If the value of *val* in the *dosomething* function changes, the value of *one* in the calling program will also change.

When a function needs to return multiple values to the calling function, *call-by-reference* arguments should be used.

Syntax for call by reference

SYNTAX RULE: Arguments which are to return a value to the calling function must be denoted by an "&" in the function prototype statement and in the function definition header.

Consider again the function which "should" return the values of length and width to the calling program. To accomplish this, we can now complete the function header as follows:

        void get_data (float& length, float& width)

The parameters are both call-by-reference so any values read for the length and width will be "returned" to the calling program.

EXERCISE 3:   Consider the program **inlab9a.cpp** again. This time, observe the program in more detail. Examine all the arguments listed in the program and indicate whether these arguments are call-by-value or call-by-reference. For all arguments that are call-by-reference, explain why you think they were set up in this way.

EXERCISE 4:   Load the file **inlab9b.cpp** to memory. This program is totally correct except that all arguments (both formal and actual) have been omitted. Replace all blanks included in the program with appropriate arguments. Don't forget the appropriate syntax for all call-by-reference arguments! Compile and run this program. A hardcopy of this program is listed below for your convenience. Turn in a listing and a run of this program.

```
//File:          inlab9b.cpp
//Author:
//Purpose:       This program will allow the user to input the
//               dimensions of a rectangle.  Then the program will
//               print a menu giving the user the choice of finding
//               1) the perimeter of a rectangle or 2) the area of a
//               rectangle.

//include files...
#include <iostream.h>

void main ()
{
    //function prototypes...
    void get_data (____,____,____);        //input all data
    float perimeter (____,____ );          //find the perimeter
    float area (____ ,____);               //find the area

    //local declarations...
    float answer;                          //stores desired computation
    float length, width;                   //length and width of rectangle
    int operation;                         //denotes desired operation
```

```
// obtain length and width of rectangle and the operation
// to be performed
get_data (_____, _____, _____);

//perform indicated operation
if (operation == 1)
{
        answer = area (_____, _____);
        cout << "The area of the rectangle with a length of ";

}
else
{
        answer = perimeter (_____, _____);
        cout << "The perimeter of the rectangle with a length of ";

}

// print calculation
cout << length << " and a width of " << width << " is :";
cout << answer << endl;

//end of main...
return;
}
```

```
//Function:      get_data()
//Purpose:       Function to print prompt and input the length and
//               width of the rectangle.  Also input is the
//               operation to be performed.

void get_data (_____,_____,_____)

{
    //IN:  no input arguments
    //OUT: returns the length and width of a rectangle
    //OUT: returns type of operation to be performed
    //RETURN VALUE: does not compute a return value

    cout << "Please enter the length and width of the rectangle";
    cout << endl;
    cin  >> len >> wid;
    cout << endl;
    cout << endl;
    cout << "1 - Compute the area of the rectangle" << endl;
    cout << "2 - Compute the perimeter of the rectangle" <<endl;
    cout << endl;
    cout << "ENTER TYPE OF OPERATION TO BE PERFORMED: ";
    cin  >> oper;
    cout << endl;
    cout << endl;
```

```
    return;
}


//Function:      perimeter()
//Purpose:       Function to compute perimeter.

float perimeter (_____, _____)
{
    //IN: length and width of rectangle
    //OUT: no return arguments
    //RETURN VALUE:  perimeter of the rectangle

    return (2 * len + 2 * wid);
}

//Function:      area()
//Purpose:       Function to compute area

float area (_____,_____)
{
    //IN:  length and width of rectangle
    //OUT:  no return arguments
    //RETURN VALUE:  area of the rectangle

    return (len * wid);
}
```

C.   Scope

Lastly in this lab, we discuss the concept of scope which deals with the visibility or usefulness of variables throughout a C++ program. Before we can understand scope, however, consider the following definitions:

> **-local variables** - We say that variables defined in a function are local variables. This means that these variables are visible and can only be used by the function in which the variable was defined!

> **-global variables** - Variables may also be defined **before** function definitions. We say that these variables are global variables. This means that these variables are visible and can be used by **ALL** functions listed after the definition of these variables in the program.

In general, it is not good practice to make use of global variables within individual functions. It is best for each function to be as self contained as possible. This can best be achieved if the function only uses variables passed as arguments or variables which are defined locally.

We will briefly study global variables in order to fully understand this aspect of C++ scope.

Consider the following program. The picture at the top is called a <u>block diagram.</u> Each function is considered to be a block and the function's local variables are drawn inside the block corresponding to the function. Since the global variables were defined before the function main, they are shown in the block diagram before the block which depicts main.

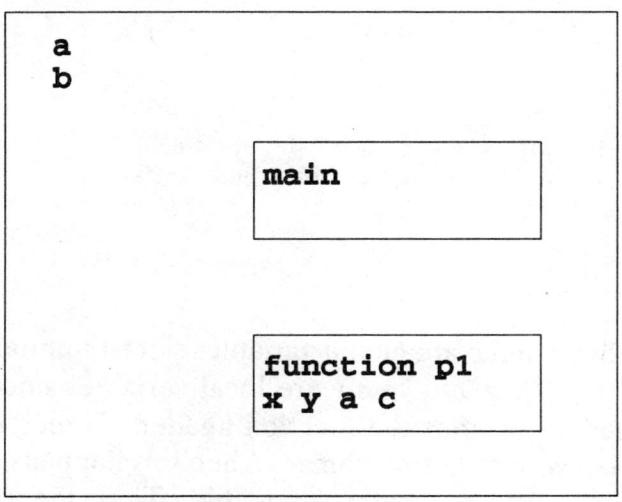

```
1      //File:           scope.cpp
2      //Author:
3      //Purpose:        This program demonstrates scope
4
5      //include files...
6      #include <iostream.h>
7
8      //global function prototypes...
9      void p1 (int& , int );
10
11     //global declarations....
12     int a,b;
13
14     void main ()
15     {
16         a = 10;
17         b = 20;
18         cout << "Before p1, a = " << a << " b = " << b << endl;
19         p1 (a,b);
20         cout << "After p1, a = " << a << " b = " << b << endl;
21
22         //end of main...
23         return;
24     }
25
```

```
26        //Function:      p1()
27        //Purpose:       Further demonstrate scope
28
29        void p1 (int& x, int y)
30        {
31
32            //local declarations...
33            int a,c;
34
35            a = 100;
36            c = 200;
37            x = 300;
38            y = 400;
39            cout << "inside p1, a = " << a << " b = " << b << endl;
40            cout << "x = " << x << " and y = " << y << endl;
41            return;
42        }
```

We can see from line 11 that *a* and *b* are global variables since their definition occurs **before** all function definitions. In *p1()*, *a*, *c*, *x* and *y* are local variables since these variables are defined in the function header or after the function header. Notice that there is a global variable and a local variable with the same name. When this happens, any reference to this name results in action being taken as locally as possible. Thus, the assignment *a = 100* in the function called *p1()* only effects the local *a* and not the global *a*. Since *a* and *b* are global variables, their scope is the entire program including the *p1()* function. Since the local variables *a*, *c*, *x* and *y* are defined in *p1()*, their scope is the function *p1()* and they are not known outside of that function.

p1() has two formal arguments *x* and *y*. The *x* argument is a call-by-reference argument and the *y* argument is a call-by-value argument.

Execution of the program is as follows:

1)   The global variables *a* and *b* receive values 10 and 20 respectively from the first two assignment statements (lines 16 and 17).

EXERCISE 5:   What is the output generated by line 18 in the program?

2)   Line 19 calls *p1()*. Since *x* is a reference argument, *x* and *a* refer to a common memory location. Since *y* is a value argument, *y* has its own location and receives the value that was stored in *b*.

GLOBAL variables   **IN p1**

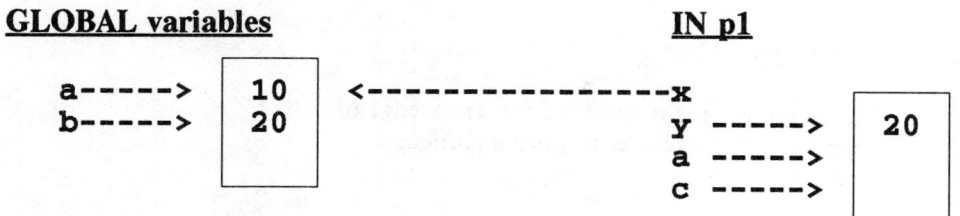

3)   *p1()* has two local variables called *a* and *c*; you can see from the diagram above that each of these receive their own memory locations. When *p1()* is first called, memory is shown above. The appearance of memory after the four assignment statements (lines 35 - 38) have been made is shown below:

GLOBAL variables   **IN p1**

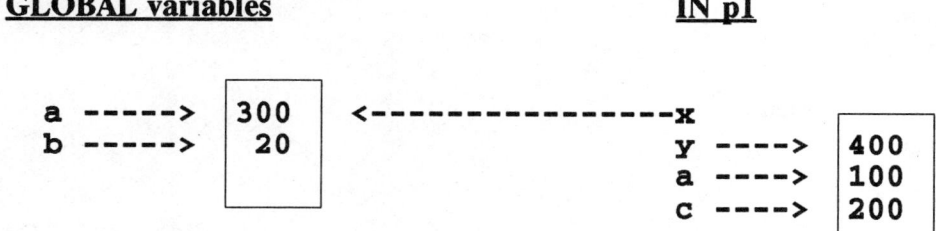

EXERCISE 6:   Predict the output generated by statements 39 and 40 in the function *p1()*. Note that *p1()* does not have a local variable called *b*, thus when a reference to *b* is made in the *cout* statement, all local variables are checked first and when *b* is not found, global variables are searched to see if there is a global variable called *b*.

EXERCISE 7:   Predict the output generated by line 20 when control is returned to the main function. Note that the value of *a* has changed because it corresponded to the variable parameter *x* in the function. The value of *b* did not change since it corresponded to the value argument *y* in the function.

EXERCISE 8:   Load the C++ program called **inlab9c.cpp** to memory and:

   a)   Draw a block diagram of the program.
   b)   Identify all global variables.
   c)   Identify all local variables in *sub_one()*.
   d)   Identify all local variables in *sub_two()*.
   e)   Identify all formal arguments in *sub_one()*.
   f)   Identify all actual arguments in the call to *sub_one()*.

The listing of this program follows for your convenience.

```
//File:         inlab9c.cpp
//Author:
//Purpose:      This is a nonsense program to test knowledge of
//              scope. It is not intended to solve a particular
//              problem.

//WARNING:      Features of C++ used in this lab are not
//              considered good programming practice and should not
//              normally be used!!!

//include files...
#include <iostream.h>

//global function prototypes...
void sub_one (int, int&);
void sub_two (void);

//global variable declarations...
int x, y, z;

void main ()
{
    x = 1;
    y = 2;
    z = 3;

    cout << "Before sub_one:  x = " << x << ", y = " << y;
    cout << " and z = " << z << endl;
    cout << endl;

    sub_one (x, y);

    cout << "After sub_one:  x = " << x << ", y = " << y;
    cout << " and z = " << z << endl;
    cout << endl;

    sub_two ();

    cout << "After sub_two:  x = " << x << ", y = " << y;
    cout << " and z = " << z << endl;
    cout << endl;

    //end of main...
    return;

}


//Function:     sub_one
//Purpose:      Further explore scope of variables

void sub_one (int a, int& b)
```

```
{
    //local declarations...
    int z, w;

    a = a + 1;
    b = a + 5;
    z = b - 1;
    w = x;

    cout << "In sub_one: x = " << x << ", y = " << y;
    cout << " and z = " << z << endl;
    cout << "In sub_one: w = " << w << ", a = " << a;
    cout << " and b = " << b << endl << endl;
    return;

}


//Function:      sub_two
//Purpose:       More scope

void sub_two (void)
{
    //local declarations...
    int a, x;

    a = 5;
    x = 10;
    y = 20;
    cout << "In sub_two:  a = " << a << ", x = " << x;
    cout << ", y = " << y << ", and z = " << z << endl;
    cout << endl;
    return;

}
```

EXERCISE 9:   Predict the output generated by the above program.

NOTE: Turn in Lab 9 answer sheets and a listing and a run of **inlab9b.cpp** (if possible on your system) for Exercise 4.

Lab 9 - Answer Sheet

NAME: _____

EXERCISE 1:

   1)   **Functions with no return value and no input arguments:**

        _____

        _____

   2)   **Functions with a return value and no input arguments:**

        _____

        _____

   3)   **Functions without a return value and with input arguments:**

        _____

        _____

   4)   **Function with a return value and with input arguments:**

        _____

        _____

   5)   **Library functions:**

        _____

        _____

EXERCISE 2:

EXERCISE 3:

EXERCISE 5:

OUTPUT:_____

EXERCISE 6:

LINE 39 OUTPUT:_____

LINE 40 OUTPUT:_____

EXERCISE 7:

LINE 20 OUTPUT:_____

EXERCISE 8:

a)

b)   global variables:_____

c)   local sub_one variables:_____

d)   local sub_two variables:_____

e)   formal arguments in sub_one:_____

f)   actual arguments in call to sub_one:_____

EXERCISE 9:

Lab 10

File Operations

<table>
<tr><td>Objectives:</td><td>To review input/output concepts
To learn how to create data files
To learn about redirection of I/O
To learn about input file functions
To learn about output file functions</td></tr>
</table>

A.   Input/Output Concepts

In previous labs we have only used C++ standard input and output devices to produce solutions to various problems. Thus the keyboard was used to enter the needed data during the execution of the program and the output of the program was displayed on the computer screen. In other words, the programmer participated in **interactive processing**, a type of processing in which the user communicates with the processor during program execution. There is a second form of processing called **batch processing**. Many programs in the "real" world use batch processing. Batch processing uses secondary storage devices (disks or tapes) from which data is obtained for input and may be used to store output data produced by a program. This type of processing is called batch processing since the user does not communicate with the processor during the program execution. If a program is executed in batch mode, then, all data could be obtained from a disk and all output could be stored on the disk as well.

EXERCISE 1:   Describe the difference between batch processing and interactive processing.

B. Creating Files

A **file** is a collection of related data items. You have been working with various files throughout this semester and, hopefully, you are now familiar with several different types of files: source files, executable files, etc. Look at this simple example of a data file called *customers.dat*:

        DOE, JOHN
        150.00
        SMITH, JIM
        270.00
        BROWN, CAROL
        800.40
        .
        .
        .

This data file consists of a person's name and charges for services rendered for a particular company. We may create this file using any editor including the IDE built-in editor in exactly the same manner as we create our source files for our C++ programs. We would load the editor and then type in the lines of data exactly as they appear above. When this information is needed by a billing program, we could specify that the computer obtain all needed data from this data file rather than from the keyboard. When the billing program is executed, the user is not required to interactively type in the above data -- all data is obtained from this data file which permanently resides on a secondary storage device.

EXERCISE 2: Why might it be beneficial to instruct C++ to obtain needed data in a program from a data file, rather than from the user at run time?

EXERCISE 3: Use the C++IDE editor to create a data file called **inlab10a.dat** which contains the following data:

        150.00
        50.00
        270.00
        20.00
        300.00
        10.99

Data files may also be created by a program. In previous lab exercises the output of a program has appeared on the standard output device, the computer screen. However, often it is beneficial to direct output to a secondary storage device instead, thus creating a data file. We will address this later in the lab.

C. Redirection of I/O

One way to associate our input and output with a batch data file instead of the standard input and output devices is through input/output redirection using operating system commands. You can instruct your C++ program, say *myprog.cpp*, to take its input from a file *mydata.dat*. We briefly state how this can be accomplished.

Suppose that we have a program called *myprog.cpp*. When we compile this program, the compiler produces an executable file called *myprog.exe* which is stored on the current drive. This is a permanent file and can be executed by typing in the name of the executable file. For example, if we assume that this file is stored on a disk in the A drive, this file can be executed under MS-DOS by typing:

a:myprog

To redirect the input, type in the following at the operating system prompt:

a:myprog < a:mydata.dat

This statement causes the program called *myprog* which is found on the A drive to execute and to obtain all input from the file on the A drive called *mydata.dat* instead of the keyboard. Since data is read from the file instead of the keyboard, the program need not supply prompting prints. Thus if your program were reading (by redirection) from the file that you created in Exercise 3, all you would need in your program would be:

cin >> amount;

This would obtain the first value from the file. The value of *amount* would be 150.00 if this were the first input statement in the C++ program.

Similarly, output may be redirected from the screen to a file, say *outfile.dat*, by using the operating system command:

a:myprog > a:outfile.dat

This would cause all output generated by any *cout* statements to be sent to the file *outfile.dat* on the disk in drive A.

EXERCISE 4:   Copy the file called *inlab10a.cpp* to your account. 1) Explain the purpose of this program and 2) tell whether this program requires user input at run time. A listing of the program follows for your convenience.

```
//Function:        inlab10a.cpp
//Author:
//Purpose:         Updates a checking account given the
//                 starting balance and the amount of the
//                 check written against the account.

//include files...
#include <iostream.h>
#include <iomanip.h>

//global function protypes...
void print_stars ();

void main ()
{
    //function prototypes...
    void heading ();                            //display bank heading
    void get_data(float&, float&);              //get balance & check amt
    float new_balance (float, float);           //calculate new balance
    char over (float);                          //determine if overdrawn
    void print_info (float, float, float, char); //display results

    //local declarations...
    float old_balance,                          //starting balance of the account
        check,                                  //amount of the check
        balance;                                //new balance
    char over_drawn;                            //Is the account over drawn? (y-yes, n-no)

    //get the starting balance and check amount
    get_data (old_balance, check);

    //calculate and print the new balance
    heading ();
    balance = new_balance (old_balance,  check) ;
    over_drawn = over (balance);
    print_info (old_balance, check, balance, over_drawn);
    print_stars ();

    //end of main...
}

//Function:        get_data()
//Purpose:         Input starting checking balance and amount of check.

void get_data (float& old,                      //OUT: starting account balance
               float& amount)                   //OUT: check amount
{
    cout << "Enter balance from previous month" ;
    cout << " and hit <ENTER>" << endl;
    cin  >> old;
    cout << "Enter amount of check and hit <ENTER>" << endl;
```

```
    cin >> amount;
    return;
}


//Function:      heading()
//Purpose:       Print a heading for the bank statement.

void heading ()
{
    cout << endl;
    cout << endl;
    cout << endl;
    print_stars ();
    print_stars ();
    cout <<"****************FIFTH NATIONAL BANK********************";
    cout << endl;
    cout << "              1515 ONE TIME STREET" << endl;
    cout << "              MANY APPLES, MINNESOTA";
    print_stars ();
    print_stars ();
    return;
}


//Function:      new_balance()
//Purpose:       Compute and return ending bank balance.

float new_balance (float old,              //IN: starting balance
                   float amount )          //IN: check amount
{
    return old - amount;
}



//Function:      over()
//Purpose:       Determine if account is overdrawn or not.

char over (float balance)                  //IN: the ending balance

{
    //local declarations...
    char overdrawn;                        //over drawn status

    if (balance < 0)
         overdrawn = 'y';
    else
         overdrawn = 'n';
    return overdrawn;
}


//Function:      print_info()
//Purpose:       Print all banking information.
```

```
void print_info (float old,                    //IN:  starting balance
                 float amount,                 //IN:  check amount
                 float bal,                    //IN:  ending balance
                 char over)                    //IN:  over drawn indicator
{
    cout << setiosflags (ios::showpoint | ios::fixed);
    cout << endl;
    cout << " OLD BALANCE  CHECK AMOUNT   NEW BALANCE  OVER DRAWN"<<endl;
    cout << endl;
    cout << setprecision (2) << setw (10) << old <<setw (15) << amount;
    cout << setw (15) << bal;
    cout << "        " << over;
    cout << endl;
    return;
}


//Function:      print_stars()
//Purpose:       Print decorative stars.

void print_stars ()
{
    cout << endl;
    cout << "********************************************************";
    cout << endl;
}
```

EXERCISE 5:   Compile and run the program **inlab10a.cpp** so that you will be familiar with the execution of the program. Now redirect the input so that it comes from the file **inlab10a.dat** which you created in Exercise 3. Note:

1)   The program should obtain all input from the file *inlab10a.dat*. Therefore, there is no need to prompt the user for input! Remove the prompts.

2)   This program reads only one data set. The data file *inlab10a.dat* contains three sets of data. Therefore, set up a loop in this program so that it will process all three sets of data.

D.   Accessing Data Files for Input

We now consider a second method of accessing data files for input. Instead of redirecting our input, we will directly access the data in an input file. In order to do this, it is necessary to first introduce the concept of the C++ stream. To help to understand a C++ *stream*, try to visualize a stream of water flowing toward a nearby lake. Similar to this stream of water, a stream in C++ is a sequence (stream or flow) of characters. Up until now, all input and output has been implemented using the standard input stream (cin) and the standard output stream (cout). Every C++ program has these streams and at least one other, the standard error stream (*cerr*) available as long as the *iostream.h* header file is included. Therefore, C++, sets up a *stream* from the keyboard so that data may *flow* from the keyboard to the input request in a given program. We use the input operator >> to extract data from the stream. The input statement

```
char one_char;
cin >> one_char;
```

will examine the input stream from the keyboard, will obtain the next non-white space character in the stream and will store this character in memory under the name, *one_char*. If no character is present in the stream, the execution pauses to wait for one. The input statement

```
int number1;
cin >> number1;
```

will examine the input stream from the keyboard for the next integer. In this example, the computer will skip any leading white space, obtain digits from the keyboard until a non-numeric character is encountered, and will store this integer in memory under the name, *number1*.

In a similar manner, we note that *cout* sets up a *stream* to the screen so that the data may *flow* from memory to the screen. The output operator << is used to put data into the stream. Therefore, we see that all input and output operations in C++ are performed using streams. Once the concept of a stream is understood, it is relatively easy to understand the changes that must be made in a C++ program in order to obtain input from another stream, NOT the standard keyboard stream.

Suppose that we have created a file called *inlab10b.dat*. Also, assume that it contains the following data:

```
45 52
88 91
```

This file consists of two lines of two integers each and can be accessed by the following C++ program:

```
//File:       inlab10b.cpp
//Author:
//Purpose:    This program is an example of a C++ program which
//            obtains input to the program from a file rather
//            than from the keyboard.  It will read integers
//            from a file called inlab10b.dat.  The program will
```

```
//                 then output the integers to the screen.

//include files...
#include <iostream.h>
#include <fstream.h>
#include <iomanip.h>

void main ()
{
    //local declarations...
    ifstream myin;              //input file stream
    int number1, number2;       //variables to hold integers read
    int i;                      //which line is being read from the file?

    //prepare file for reading and identify external file
    myin.open ("inlab10b.dat");

    //loop to read data
    for (i=1; i<3; i++)
    {
        myin >> number1 >> number2;
        cout << "Line " << i << ": " << setw(7) << number1;
        cout << setw (7) << number2 << endl;
    }

    //end of main...
    return;
}
```

There are several directives which MUST be included in a C++ program in order to access a data file. They are shown in bold above. The above program demonstrates that we MUST:

1)   inform the compiler that we wish to use an input stream other than the standard input stream. This was accomplished by the statement
        ifstream myin;
      which declares *myin* to be an input file stream. The type, *ifstream*, is defined in the C++ library header file *fstream.h*. Thus this header file must be included using: *#include <fstream.h>*.

2)   once *myin* has been declared to be an input stream, the file must be prepared for reading. We use the open function to do this:
        myin.open ("inlab10b.dat");
      This statement uses the *open* function which attaches the input stream *myin* to the external file *inlab10b.dat*. Thus the stream is now open, has an associated buffer, and the data it will receive will originate from a file called *inlab10b.dat*.

3) obtain the desired input. Remember that "cin" is the function which allows one to access the standard input stream. Now, we wish to obtain input from the stream, *myin*, established above. Thus we use:

myin >> number1 >> number2;

This statement will extract two integers from the stream called *myin*.

EXERCISE 6: Make all necessary changes in **inlab10a.cpp** so that data is obtained from the data file called *inlab10a.dat* which you created in Exercise 3. Do not use redirection of input. Add statements to your C++ program so that each input comes from the file by using file functions.

EXERCISE 7: Compile and execute this program. DO NOT PROCEED TO THE NEXT STEP UNTIL THIS PROGRAM EXECUTES PROPERLY!

Now, let's try reading characters from a file. Suppose that we have previously created a data file called *namefile.dat* which contains an undetermined number of employee names with one name on each line of the data file. Consider the following program.

```
//File:          inlab10c.cpp
//Author:
//Purpose:       This program will read data from an external file called
//               namefile.dat. Output is to the screen.

//include files..
#include <fstream.h>
#include <iostream.h>

void main ()
{
    //local declarations...
    const char eoln = '\n';      //eoln is the end-of-line character
    int k;                        //count the number of names
    char letter;                  //a single character of a name
    ifstream filein;              //declare the input file stream

    //open the input stream
    filein.open("namefile.dat");

    k = 1;
    filein.get (letter);

    //Outer loop reads until end-of-file
    while (!filein.eof())
    {
        cout << "NAME " << k << ": ";
```

```
            //Inner loop reads one line (one name)
            while ((letter != eoln) && (!filein.eof ()))
            {
                cout << letter;
                filein.get (letter);
            }
            cout << endl;
            k++;
            filein.get (letter);
        }
        k--;
        cout << "There were " << k << " names in the file.";
        cout << endl;

        //end of main...
        return;
}
```

This program contains the new functions, *get()* and *eof()*.

The function *get()* is a stream input function which reads one character at a time and may be used with any stream. See the program above for the syntax of *get()*. Using the function *get()*, whitespace characters are treated just like all other characters. Thus when a blank or a newline is encountered in the input stream, it is read from the stream just like any other character.

The function *eof()* is a another example of a stream input function. *eof()* returns the value true or false. If the end-of-file has been reached, then *eof()* returns the value true. Otherwise, *eof()* is false. See the lines in bold above. Note that the *eof()* function is used in this example in both of the while loops. This is a common method for obtaining data when the exact number of data items is not known.

EXERCISE 8:   This program contains TWO while loops. What is the purpose of the OUTSIDE while loop? What is the purpose of the INSIDE while loop? Why is the second part of the inside while condition (i.e. *!filein.eof()*)) necessary?

E.   Accessing Data Files for Output

We indicated earlier in this lab that a text file may be created by the user or by program output. This can be accomplished by allowing a C++ program to send output to a file rather than to the screen. We mentioned that data could be sent to an output file by using redirection. It can also be sent to an output file directly which is the subject of this section.

The following program creates a permanent file called *inlab10d.dat*.

```
//File:           inlab10d.cpp
//Author:
//Purpose:        This program will read in names and phone numbers.
//                It creates a permanent file called inlab10d.dat
//                on the disk in the default drive.  The program will
//                continue to read in names and phone numbers until
//                the user indicates end of file.

//include files...
#include <iostream.h>
#include <fstream.h>

void main ()
{
    //local declarations...
    const eoln = '\n';                       //the new line character
    ofstream out_data ("inlab10d.dat");      //output file stream
    char one_char;                           //a single character

    //process the file of names and numbers
    cout << "Please enter a name and hit <ENTER>." << endl;
    cin.get (one_char);
    while (!cin.eof ())
    {
        //get a name and put it in the file
        while (one_char != eoln)
        {
            out_data.put (one_char);
            cin.get (one_char);
        }
        out_data.put (eoln);
        cout << "Please enter the corresponding phone number";
        cout << " and hit <ENTER>." << endl;
        cin.get (one_char);

        //get a phone number and put it in the file
        while ( one_char != eoln)
        {
            out_data.put (one_char);
            cin.get (one_char);
        }
        out_data.put (eoln);

        //are there any more to process?
        cout << "If you have more data, please type in name";
        cout << " and hit <ENTER>." << endl;
        cout << "Hit CONTROL Z and hit <ENTER> if there is no more data.";
        cout << endl;
        cin.get (one_char);
    }
```

```
    out_data.put (one_char);

    //end of main...
    return;
}
```

Note the stream function *put()* in the program above. This function is used for writing a character into the stream which in this case is the file called *inlab10d.dat*. The end of line character ('\n') was stored in the file so that the file contains only one name or phone number per line.

Another method for writing data to a file is very similar to the standard output discussed in earlier labs. As a review, note that the statement:

```
    cout << "HELLO";
    cout << endl;
```

sends the string of characters "HELLO" to the standard output stream, usually the screen. The statement,

```
    out_data << "HELLO";
    out_data << endl;
```

will send the string of characters "HELLO" to the stream called *out_data* which we have defined to be an output stream corresponding to a file called *inlab10d.dat* in the above program.

Exercise 9: Copy the file *inlab10d.cpp* to your account and add code so that a person's age is also stored permanently in the file. Be sure to store the end of line character ('\n') in the file after the person's age so that the file contains only one piece of information on each line.

Exercise 10: Compile and execute the revised *inlab10d.cpp* program. During execution, type in data for at least three people. Type in your name, phone and age first.

Lab 10 - Answer Sheet

NAME:_____

EXERCISE 1:

Batch processing is _____

_____.

Interactive processing is _____

_____.

EXERCISE 2:

Why might it be beneficial to instruct the computer to
obtain data from a file?

_____

_____.

EXERCISE 4:

Purpose:_____

_____

_____

Does this program require user input?_____

EXERCISE 8:

What is the purpose of the OUTSIDE while loop?

_____

_____

What is the purpose of the INSIDE while loop?

_____

_____

Why is the second part of the inside while loop (!filein.eof()) necessary?

_____

_____

Lab 11

One-Dimensional Arrays

Objectives:	Introduce basic concepts of one-dimensional arrays
	Introduce an array search
	Introduce common array errors

A. Basic Concepts

We have found previously that C++ has simple data types (float, char, and int). These simple data types do not provide a way to store large amounts of data. Today's lab will introduce data types provided in C++ and other programming languages called structured data types. C++ provides two such types: the array and the structure (or struct). Today's lab will address the concept of storing large amounts of data using an array.

What is an array?

To understand what an array is, we first review what a variable is. A variable is a symbolic name for a specific location in main memory. For example, the statements

$$int \ x;$$
.
.
$$x = 25;$$

instruct the computer to set aside a memory location which will hold an integer, giving the memory location the symbolic name *x*. The second statement instructs the computer to store the integer 25 in the memory location symbolized by the variable *x*.

How can we store twenty integers in memory? We could dream up twenty different symbolic names, such as *x1, x2, x3, ..., x20*, for twenty places in memory. Obviously, this is not convenient. C++ has a structured data type called an array which addresses this particular problem.

An **array**, then, is a group of locations in memory such that a) the locations are usually consecutive, b) all locations contain the same type of data and c) all locations are referenced by the same symbolic name.

Why do we need an array type?

Hopefully, from the previous discussion you can see that arrays are used anytime we wish to store and manipulate more than a few pieces of data of the same type. Consider the following examples:

1.   Suppose that we want to print out 30 integers in reverse order. We need to use an array for this application because we **must** remember all 30 numbers in order to print them out in reverse.

2.   Suppose that we wish to compute the average pay for 30 people. We do not require an array for this application, since we do not need to remember the data for all 30 people. In this problem we input data for one person and add it to an accumulator. We can use the same variables for the next person, since we no longer need to remember data for the previous person.

Let's look at each of the following problems and determine if an array should be used.

1.   Print a list of 30 numbers in ascending order assuming the numbers are entered in random order. Yes, arrays should be used since we must **remember** all of the numbers before we can rearrange them so they can be printed.

2.   Read in 30 grades, compute the average of the grades and then print the number of grades above and below the average. Yes, arrays must be used. In order to solve this problem we must read and keep all of the numbers. After we find the average, we must re-examine the grades and count them according to whether they are above or below the average.

EXERCISE 1:   In each of the following situations, determine whether an array would be necessary.

a)   Read in 100 test scores and find the largest score.

b)   Calculate the median of 50 test scores (this is the test score for which half of the scores are above and half the scores are below). The scores are entered in random order.

How are arrays declared?

Now that we know when to use arrays, we need to study C++ array syntax. First, we must learn how to declare a structured type called an array. Suppose we need an array to store 30 real numbers.

```
const size = 30;
float list [size];
```

Note the use of the constant *size* for the upper limit on the size of the array. Using const values to denote the size of the array is not required but is a good programming practice. This code causes 30 locations in memory to be set aside under the name *list*.

EXERCISE 2:   Load the file called **inlab11.cpp** to memory. This file is included at the end of the lab for your convenience. Insert declaration statements where indicated to declare the following array types and variable names.

1.   The variable *numbers* to store 10 integers.
2.   The variable *listofvalues* to store 5 real numbers.

How are arrays accessed?

In order to store information in an array, one must:

1.   Specify the name of the array and
2.   Specify exactly which location in the array is to be used.

We specify locations in the array by using **subscripts**. For example reconsider our array *list* defined above. list[1] = 20; means, look at the location designated 1 in the array list and store the value 20 in this position. The subscript can be a constant, variable or expression as shown below :

```
list[5*2] = 20; i.e., subscript = 10
list[x] = 20;  i.e., subscript = the value of the variable x
```

To determine valid values for the subscript, reconsider the definition of the array:

float list [size];

The upper limit of the subscripts is calculated from the value in the brackets, namely *size - 1*. In C++, the lower limit is always 0. Thus the subscript may vary from 0 to size - 1. Thus the first memory location assigned to list is designated by the first subscript 0, the second by 1, and so on, up to the last one which is designated by the subscript *size - 1*. If, instead, list were declared as follows:

float list [size + 1];

then we could access list[0], list[1], ..., list[size].

Now consider *inlab11.cpp* again. The function *get_numbers()* demonstrates how an array is typically read into memory. A loop of some kind is used to vary the subscript of the array from the first value to the last value to be read.

Note the argument list in the *get_numbers()* function:

```
void get_numbers (int numbers[],    //OUT: List to be read
                  int size)         //IN:  How many in the list
```

It includes two formal arguments: the array, called *numbers*, which is to be filled with values by the function; and the number of values, *size*, which is sent to the function. Note how the array *numbers* is declared!

WARNING 1: All arrays in C++ are call-by-reference parameters. This means that when an array appears in an actual argument list, the address of the first element in the array is sent to the function, not the contents of the array! Therefore, the array in the formal argument list will be an alias (will refer to) the same array as the actual argument.

WARNING 2: Use a reserve word *const* in a formal argument list if an array is used **and** the contents of the array **should NOT** be altered. As an example, consider the following function header:

void print_numbers (int size, const int numbers [])

The values in the array *numbers* will not change in the *print_numbers()* function because we have used *const* in the formal argument list. Therefore, we can protect the contents of the array by using *const*.

EXERCISE 3:   We will now modify *inlab11.cpp* in order to read in values into the array *listofvalues* which we declared in Exercise 2 above. Add the following function to this program:

A function called *get_list()* which will read in 5 real numbers and store them in an array called *listofvalues*.

EXERCISE 4: Consider the function called ***print_numbers***, and note how it prints out each number in the array *numbers*, one per line. Insert the following additional function into *inlab11.cpp*:

A function called *print_list()* which will print out the numbers stored in the array called listofvalues in reverse order one per line. Hint: the loop must start with 4 and count down to 0.

EXERCISE 5: Add statements to the main function to call the two new functions written in Exercises 3 and 4 above. Compile and run your updated version of **inlab11.cpp** before you go on to the next exercise. Enter any data that you wish for the arrays.

B. Searching an Array

Arrays are extremely useful in many situations. Some of the most common applications for arrays include: traversing (looking at) a list, searching a list, and sorting a list.

We have already traversed a list when we printed it. Now, we consider searching an array. Searching an array refers to the concept of looking for a particular data item in an array. One easy method for accomplishing this is to set up a loop which will sequentially look at each element in the array. Hence, this method of searching is called a **sequential search**. Consider the following function :

```
//Function: search ()
//Purpose:  Search the array, a, for value.
//          Return the location of  value or return -1
//          to indicate that value was not found.

int search (int value,          //IN: value to be searched
            int a[],            //IN: a is the array to be searched
            int size)           //IN: number of elements in the array to be searched
{
        int position=-1;         //initialize the returned position
        for (int i=0; i< size; i++)
                if (value == a[i])
                        position = i;
        return position;
}
```

This function receives three values: *value* is the number we will be searching for, *a* is the array to be searched, and *size* is the number of locations contained in the array. This function performs a sequential search and returns the position of the value in the array or -1 if the value is not found. This procedure will waste a lot of computer time unless we are seeking the last occurrence of *value* since it continues to search even after it finds the value the first time. Inserting a flag is useful here. A **flag** is a concept in computer science which helps the programmer to know whether a certain condition has occurred or not.

Flags must :

      1. Be initialized
      2. Be reset if needed and
      3. Be examined

to be useful.

Consider the following updated version of *search()*:

```
//Function: search
//Purpose:  Search the array, a, for value.
//          Return the location of  value or return -1
//          to indicate that value was not found.

int search (int value,          //IN: search for value
            int a[],            //IN: a is the array to be searched
            int size)           //IN: number of elements in the array to be searched
{
        int i=-1;               //initialize the returned position
        int found;              //flag which indicates when value is found

        //initialize the flag
        found = false;          //must include the <stdio.h> library for this assignment!

        // perform the search
        do
        {
                i++;
                if value == a[i]
                        found = true;
        }
        while (!(found) && (i <size));
        return i;
}
```

In the above function the flag *found* is initialized to false. This means, we have not found the number that we are looking for yet. Secondly, *found* is reset to true when the value is found in the array. This means we have now found the value we are looking for and we should discontinue the search. Lastly, the search is terminated if the value is found (our flag is true) or if we have run out of places to look for it.

EXERCISE 6: Using the above sequential search as a guide, insert a function called *find_and_print()* into *inlab11.cpp*. This function should search the array *numbers* for values from the array *listofvalues* (truncated to integer). Print messages to indicate where each value is found in the array *numbers* or to indicate that a value was not found. i.e. Look at the first value that is stored in the array called *listofvalues*. Truncate it to make it an integer. Then search the array called *numbers* and print out a message explaining whether that value is contained in *numbers* or not. If it is, print out where (the index or position) it was found. If it is not, print out a message so stating. Then look at the next value in *listofvalues* and continue in this fashion. HINT: You need two loops as follows.

```
int value;
.

.
for (j = 0; j < 5; j++)
{
        value = listofvalues[j] + .5;
        do
        {
            .

            .
        }
        while etc.
        .


}
```

EXERCISE 7: Compile and run the above program. Submit a listing, compile and run of the above program. Make sure your name is included in the comments.

C. Array Errors

There are several errors that are typically made by beginning programmers using arrays. Among them are:

1) Trying to inspect an array subscript that is out of range. For example, suppose the following declarations have been set up:

```
const howmany = 10;
int list [howmany];
```

The following statement will cause some unpredictable results since this array has subscripts valued from 0 through 9!!

```
cout <<list[10];
```

We call this an **index out of bounds** error.

2)   Using parentheses instead of brackets. EXAMPLE:

```
int list (5);
or
list(1) = 5;
```

3)   Using incompatible types.
EXAMPLE:

```
int list[5];
.
.
list[1] = 1.589;
```

The right operand of the assignment should be integer, not a floating point number.

Lab 11 Files

```cpp
//File:          inlab11.cpp
//Authors:
//Purpose:       This program will read and print ten integers
//               and five floating point numbers.

//include files...
#include <iostream.h>

void main ()
{
    //const declarations...
    ***place answers to exercise 2 here!!!

    //function prototypes...
    void get_numbers ( int [], int);
    void print_numbers (int [], int);

    //local declaration...
    ***place answers to exercise 2 here!!!

    //call functions
    get_numbers (numbers, 10);
    print_numbers (numbers, 10);

    //end of main
    return;
}


//Function:      get_numbers
//Purpose:       This function reads values into an integer array.

void get_numbers (int numbers [],        //OUT: the array of integers
                  int size)              //IN:  the size of the array
{
    cout << "Please enter " << size << " numbers that you wish";
    cout << " to do manipulations with.  Thank you" << endl;
    cout << endl;

    //read in the array
    for (int i = 0; i < size; i++)
    {
        cout << "Please enter number " << i+1 << ":" << endl;
        cin >> numbers [i];
        cout << endl;
    }
    return;
}
```

```
//Function:      print_numbers
//Purpose:       This function prints the values in an integer array
//               of numbers.

void print_numbers (int numbers [],        //IN:  the array of integers
                    int size)              //IN:  the size of the array
{
    cout << endl << endl;
    cout << "This is a list of the " << size
        << " numbers as read";
    cout << endl << endl;
    for (int i = 0; i < size; i++)
    {
        cout << "NUMBER " << i + 1 << " = " << numbers [i];
        cout << endl;
    }
    return;
}
```

Lab 11 - Answer Sheet

NAME:_____

EXERCISE 1:

      a)   _____

      b)   _____

Lab 12

Character Data Revisited

Objectives:	Learn about available character functions
	Introduce character strings
	Discuss commonly used string functions

A. Character Data Type

In Lab 3, we introduced the character data type which could hold a single character value. Thus, we have been able to declare constants and variables as follows:

> const char asterisk = '*';
> char letter;
> letter = 'a';

We saw in Lab 3 that we can also input and output character data.

Character values may also be compared using the relational operators <, <=, >, >=, ==, !=. To understand the result of a comparison such as this, we must know something about the way characters are stored in the computer. Each character is assigned its own unique numeric code. The code is then changed to a binary number and the binary number is stored in a character memory location.

A common encoding scheme for character data is ASCII which stands for American Standard Code for Information Interchange. If we examine an ASCII chart, we will see that the digit characters '0' through '9' have code values of 48 through 57. The order relationship below holds for digit characters regardless of the encoding scheme:

$$'0' < '1' < ... < '8' < '9'$$

In ASCII, the uppercase characters 'A' to 'Z' have the codes 65 through 90. The relationship below holds for uppercase characters:

$$'A' < 'B' < ... < 'Y' < 'Z'$$

Similarly, the lowercase letters are ordered as:

$$'a' < 'b' < ... < 'y' < 'z'$$

In ASCII, the lowercase letters have the codes 97 through 122 so using this encoding scheme, an uppercase letter is "less than" a lowercase letter.

When we wish to discover the code used for a given character, we can use the type cast operator **int**. Thus int('0') is the value 48, int('A') is the value 65, and int('a') is the value 97 if ASCII is the encoding scheme.

Similarly, the type cast operator **char** will produce a character whose code is the given integer. Thus char(65) is 'A', char(48) is '0', etc.

EXERCISE 1:   Evaluate the following C++ expressions using the ASCII character set.

    a)   int('a') - int('A')
    b)   char(int('L'))
    c)   int('8') - int('3')

Several character functions are provided in C++ to aid in the manipulation of character data. To use these library functions the header file, *ctype.h*, must be included in a C++ program. A few of these are listed below:

Function	Purpose
tolower(c)	If c is uppercase, the function returns the corresponding lowercase letter. Otherwise, c is returned.
toupper(c)	the opposite of tolower(c)
isalpha(c)	Returns a nonzero value if c is an upper or lower case letter. Otherwise 0 is returned.
isdigit(c)	Returns a nonzero value if c is a digit. Otherwise 0 is returned.
islower(c)	Returns a nonzero value if c is a lowercase letter; otherwise 0

is returned

isupper(c)	Returns a nonzero value if c is an uppercase letter; otherwise 0 is returned.
isspace(c)	Returns nonzero if c is a space, newline, formfeed, carriage return, tab, or vertical tab. Otherwise 0 is returned.

EXERCISE 2: These functions are not difficult to write. Load the source file *inlab12a.cpp* into your account. This file contains a function *change_to_upper()* which changes an uppercase letter to a lowercase letter. It might be similar to the C++ library function *toupper()*.

EXERCISE 3: Examine the function *change_to_upper()*.

a) What are the input arguments (if any)?
b) What are the output arguments (if any)?
c) What value is returned by the function?

EXERCISE 4: Write a main program to test the function *change_to_upper()*. Turn in a listing and run of the program.

We saw in Lab 3 that *cin* and *cout* could be used to read and write character values. When reading character values using *cin*, any leading white space (blanks, tab, newline, etc.) is skipped until the first nonwhite space character is found.

For example, if the input is: ♭♭♭♭jk   (♭ is a blank)
Then, the line: *cin >> ch;*
causes the blanks to be skipped and the character *j* is read into *ch*.

We can ask C++ not to skip white space on input by setting a format state flag. The following C++ statement would cause the flag **skipws** to be turned *off* (it defaults to *on* which means that white space is ignored):

        cin.unsetf(ios::skipws);

After the flag is turned off, if the input were: ♭♭♭♭jk
Then, the line: *cin >> ch;*
causes *ch* to contain a blank since white space is no longer skipped.

C++ also provides two functions to allow one to input and output one character at a time with white space treated the same way as any other character. The two functions provided are *get()* and *put()* which we previously discussed in Lab 10. If *get()* instead of *cin* in the above example were used as:

```
char ch;
cin.get(ch);
```

and if the input were: b̷b̷b̷b̷jk

a blank would be placed in the memory location *ch*.

B. Character Strings

Until now, our use of character data has been quite limited. We often wish to store a string of characters like a name or social security number. In C++, strings of characters are stored in one-dimensional arrays of type char, one character per array element. When we have placed a string of characters in double quotes in our output instructions, we have used C++ strings. For example:

```
     cout << "Enter the test score:";
  or
     cout << "The values are ";
```

Thus a string of characters contained in double quotes is a character string. Each character string is stored as an array. Thus the string "x=" is stored as

x	=	\0
0	1	2

A string is terminated by the special character '\0' called the null character. The null character marks the end of a character string.

Thus the character string "x" is stored as an array

x	\0	. . . . . .
0	1	

while the character 'x' is stored as a single character

x

Notice the string is enclosed in double quotes while the character is enclosed in apostrophes.

A character array is used to store a character string. For example:

```
char last_name[10] = "Jackson";
```

would cause the array, *last_name* to contain:

J	a	c	k	s	o	n	\0	?	?
0	1	2	3	4	5	6	7	8	9

If instead, we had initialized last_name as:

```
char last_name[10] = "Washington";
```

then no error message would be generated in C++ but the following would occur:

W	a	s	h	i	n	g	t	o	n	\0		
0	1	2	3	4	5	6	7	8	9	.	.	.

Notice that the null character is placed at the end of the string--however, not enough space was allocated for the array and unpredictable results are likely to occur. Perhaps other valuable data may be overwritten.

EXERCISE 5:   Show a declaration of a string variable large enough to contain your first name (plus the null character). Initialize the variable to contain your first name. Show the internal representation of your name.

Input of Strings

When reading a string variable, we could use the *get()* routine described above. For example:

```
char line[80];
char ch, nwlin='\n';
int char_count=0;

//read a line of text into the character
//array line.  If the line is too long,
//only read the first 79 characters

cin.get(ch);
while ((ch != nwlin) && (char_count < 79))
{
        line[char_count]=ch;
        char_count++;
```

```
                    cin.get(ch);
        }

        //place the null terminating character in the last
        //position
        line[char_count]='\0';
```

Alternately, the *cin* function can be used to read in a string. *cin* behaves similar to the way it does when numeric data is read. Beginning white space characters (blanks, newline, tab, etc) are ignored, then all characters up to the first white space character are read and placed in the variable. When the first white space character is encountered, reading terminates and the null character is placed in the string. For example, if we have:

> *char name[20];*
> *cout << "Please enter the name "*
> *cin >> name;*

and our input is : Mouse, Mickey

then internally, name will contain:

M	o	u	s	e	,	\0	??????
0	1	2	3	4	5	6	7...19

The same input would occur no matter how many blanks, tabs, etc preceded Mouse. As you can see, the first white space terminates the string. We must remember to use the white space as a separator of data items. For example, if we read

> *cin >> name >> test;*

where *test* is an int variable and our input were

> James95

then the **name** would contain:

J	a	m	e	s	9	5	\0	????????
0	1	2	3	4	5	6	7	8....19

and the variable *test* would not have been read.

Output of Strings

A string can be printed a character at a time using the *put()* function or using *cout*. Alternately, the string can be printed all at once using cout. Assume **name** is a character string initialized as follows:

    char name[15] = "Washington";

The output
    cout <<endl<<name;

would cause the string "Washington" to be printed in the leftmost 10 positions of a new line. The instruction:

    cout << setw(15) << name;

would cause "Washington" to be printed right justified in a field of width 15 with 5 preceding blanks. To left justify the name, we could use

    cout << setiosflags(ios::left) << setw (15) << name;

This would cause "Washington" to be printed left-justified with 5 blanks after the name.

EXERCISE 6:   Load *inlab12b.cpp* to memory. This program has two string variables, *first* and *last*. The program inputs values into the two variables and prints the names. Test the program with your name after you have examined it. Modify the program so that it prints the first and last name as **last, first**. Turn in a listing and run of the modified program.

Comparison of Strings

C++ provides an extensive collection of functions which allow the programmer to manipulate strings. To use these functions, the *string.h* header file must be included in your program.

The function *strcmp()* has been provided to compare two strings, say *str1* and *str2*. If *str1* < *str2* (based on a character by character, left to right, comparison), a value less than 0 is returned. If *str1* and *str2* are the same, a value of 0 is returned and if *str1* > *str2*, a value greater than 0 is returned. The function makes character comparisons of the elements in *str1* and *str2* starting with the 0th character. It stops when it finds characters that are not equal or when it reaches the end of one of the strings.

Examples:

strcmp("A", "B")	returns < 0
strcmp("James", "Jami")	returns < 0 since 'e'<'i'
strcmp("135", "24")	returns < 0 since '1'<'2'
strcmp("ABCD","ABC")	returns > 0
strcmp("ABC","ABCD")	returns < 0
strcmp("89", "89")	returns 0

EXERCISE 7:   For each of the following string comparisons, would *strcmp* return 0, a value less than 0 or a value greater than 0?

    a)   strcmp ("158", "435")
    b)   strcmp ("abc", "ABC")
    c)   strcmp ("Jim", "Jimmy")
    d)   strcmp ("Justin", "Justin")

Copying a String

String assignment (or string copy) is achieved by the function **strcpy**. This function has two arguments, a source string and a destination string. The function copies the source string into the destination string. No check is made to determine whether or not the destination string has enough space. All characters from the source up to and including the '\0' are copied.

Example: char name[15];
                       strcpy(name, "Mr. Mouse");
would cause name to contain:

M	r	.		M	o	u	s	e	\0	?	?	?	?	?
0	1	2	3	4	5	6	7	8	9	10	11	12	13	14

If the source string is shorter than the destination string, the remaining characters in the destination string remain unchanged. If the source string is longer than the destination string, storage locations following those allocated to the destination string will be overwritten. This may cause surprising (and hard to debug) results.

String Length

C++ provides a function which returns the number of characters in a string (up to but not including the null character).

Example: strlen("Mr. Mouse") would return the value 9.

EXERCISE 8:   Show the internal representation of *str1* and the value of the variable *length* after each of the following statements, given the declarations:

```
char str1[5];
int length;
```

a)   strcpy(str1, "Joe");
        length = strlen(str1);
b)   strcpy(str1, "Joseph");
        length = strlen(str1);

EXERCISE 9:   Suppose the C++ function *strlen* did not already exist. Write a function to determine the length of a string, *str*. Write a main program to test your function. Turn in a listing and run of your program.

You can look at the help pages in Turbo C++ for the string functions by selecting the **HELP** menu. Under help, select **CONTENTS**, then select **FUNCTIONS**. Read the directions to answer the following exercise.

EXERCISE 10:   Using the **HELP** menu, find out which string function you would use to do the following. Find the name of the function and what value is returned by the functions:

a)   Find the first occurrence of a character, say **ch**, in a string, say **s.**

b)   Find the first occurrence of the string **s1** in the string **s2.**

Lab 12 Files

```
//Function:        inlab12a.cpp
//Purpose:         This function receives a character.  If it is a
//                 lowercase letter, the function returns the
//                 corresponding uppercase letter.  Otherwise, the
//                 character which is returned is the original
//                 character.

char change_to_upper (char ch)                    //the character to be changed
{
    //local declarations...
    //Define the conversion factor between a lowercase and
    //an uppercase letter. The ASCII collating sequence is
    //assumed.
    int con_factor = int ('a') - int ('A');
    char new_ch;                                   //character to return

    //Is ch a lowercase letter?
    if ((ch >= 'a') && (ch <= 'z'))
        new_ch = ch - con_factor;
    else
        new_ch = ch;

    //return the results
    return new_ch;

}
```

```
//File:          inlab12b.cpp
//Authors:
//Purpose:       This program reads and prints a person's
//               name.

//include files...
#include <iostream.h>

void main()
{
    //local declarations...
    char last[15],            //last name
         first[15];           //first name

    //Get the person's name
    cout << "\n\nPlease enter your first and last name ";
    cout << "separated by a blank space:\n";
    cin >> first >> last;

    //Display the person's name
    cout << "The person's name is: " << first << " " << last << '\n';

    //end of main...
    return;
}
```

Lab 12 - Answer Sheet

Name:_____

EXERCISE 1:

a)

b)

c)

EXERCISE 3:

a)   **Input arguments:**_____

b)   **Output arguments:**_____

c)   **Value returned:**_____

EXERCISE 5:

EXERCISE 7:

    a)

    b)

    c)

    d)

EXERCISE 8:

    a)

    b)

EXERCISE 10:

    a)   **Name of the function:** _____

          What value is returned?

    b)   **Name of the function:** _____

          What value is returned?

Lab 13
Two-Dimensional Arrays

Objective:	To introduce the concept of two-dimensional arrays
	To show C++ syntax for two-dimensional arrays
	To practice two-dimensional array manipulation

Two-dimensional arrays, the most common multidimensional arrays, are used to store information that we normally represent in table form. Examples of applications involving two-dimensional arrays include: a seating plan for a room (organized by rows and columns), a monthly budget (organized by category and month), and a grade book where rows might correspond to individual students and columns to student scores.

A. Declaration of Two-Dimensional Arrays

Example: The following declarations set aside storage for a two-dimensional array called *labscores* which contains 40 rows and 14 columns. Rows correspond to a particular student and columns correspond to a particular lab score.

const int MAXSTUDENTS=40;
const int MAXLABS=14;

int labscores [MAXSTUDENTS][MAXLABS];

EXERCISE 1:   Show C++ statements to do declare a two-dimensional array which can be used to store a yearly budget. Each row of the array corresponds to a particular budgeted item like rent, electric, etc. There are at most 15 items to be budgeted. Each column of the array corresponds to a month, January, February, etc. Of course there are 12 columns corresponding to the 12 months of the year. Data to be placed in the array consists of real numbers.

Manipulation of a two-dimensional array requires the manipulation of two subscripts or indices. When the two-dimensional array *labscores* is declared, enough storage is set aside to hold a table containing 40 rows and 14 columns for a total of 40 * 14 = 560 integer values. To access one particular value, we must specify the row and column. The row subscript ranges from 0 to MAXSTUDENTS-1 (39) and the column subscript ranges from 0 to MAXLABS-1 (13). Thus the table can be visualized as:

This two-dimensional array may also be visualized as a one-dimensional array of arrays. An alternative view of this array would be:

This two-dimensional array may be viewed as a one-dimensional array having 40 elements where each element is an array of 14 values.

B. Accessing an Array Element

In our lab scores example, suppose we wish to indicate that the second student (corresponding to row 1) made a 90 on lab 10 (corresponding to column 9). We might use the statement:

>   *labscores [1][9] = 90;*

Array subscripts may be integer constants (as in the above example), variables, or expressions. They should be within the bounds of the array.

C. Array Initialization

We can declare and initialize an array A as follows:

```
//declaration
int A[3][4] =   {{8, 2, 6, 5},          //row 0
                 {6, 3, 1 ,0},          //row 1
                 {8, 7, 9, 6}};         //row 2
```

Memory for the array may be visualized as:

A	0	1	2	3
0	8	2	6	5
1	6	3	1	0
2	8	7	9	6

EXERCISE 2:
a.   Draw an alternative visualization of memory for the array *A* as we did above for our lab scores example.
b.   What value is stored in row 2, column 1?
c.   Give the name of the location where 0 is stored?

We may also initialize an array by reading from an input file stream. Suppose we wish to read entries from an input file stream (called *myin*) into our *labscores* array. We should use two loops - one to control the student (row) and one to control the lab (column). To read in all labs corresponding to the first student, then read in all labs corresponding to the second student, and so on, we might use the following function:

```
//Function:  read_scores()
//Purpose:   This function inputs lab scores for
//           students in a computing class.
//
void read_scores (int labscores [MAXSTUDENTS][MAXLABS],    //OUT: student labs
                  int& num_students,                       //IN:  Number of students
                  int& num_labs,                           //IN:  Number of labs
                  ifstream& myin)                          //IN:  Input file stream
{

        //local variables
        int student, lab;          //which student and lab is being processed

        //first read the number of students and labs
        //stored in the file.

        myin >> num_students >> num_labs;

        //Outer loop controls which student (row) is being read
        for (student = 0; student < num_students; student++)

                //Inner loop controls which lab (column) is being read
                for (lab = 0; lab < num_labs; lab++)
                    myin >> labscores [student][lab];

        return;
}
```

EXERCISE 3:   Suppose we wish to read in the data for our students' scores but the file is organized differently. Instead of all of one student's labs appearing first, the file has all grades on lab 1 first, then all grades on lab 2, etc. How must the code above be changed to accommodate this new arrangement of data? Explain the difference on the answer sheet.

D. Function Arguments which are Two-dimensional Arrays

As with one-dimensional arrays, a two-dimensional array is automatically passed as a call-by-reference parameter. Consider the function heading above. The following function heading also could have been used:

```
void read_scores (int labscores[][MAXLABS],    //OUT: student labs
                  int& num_students,            //IN:  Number of students
                  int& num_labs,                //IN:  Number of labs
                  ifstream& myin);              //IN:  Input file stream
```

Notice the difference between these two function headings. For the *labscores* array, the second heading does not include the number of rows required by the array but does include the number of columns. The explanation is simple, when we pass an array, the compiler need only know the size of its elements, not how many elements it has. As explained above, a two-dimensional array can be thought of as a one-dimensional array of elements (which just happen to be arrays themselves). Thus the compiler needs to know the size of one of the elements. Each element is a row of values so the compiler needs to know the type of elements and how many values (the number of columns) are in each row.

If one wants to print the entire set of scores, a nested loop similar to that above would be used.

EXERCISE 4: Load the program *inlab13.cpp* and the data file *inlab13.dat*. This program contains declarations for the *labscores* array and contains a function which reads in data into this array from the file *inlab13.dat*.

a. How does this function read in the data? (all data for the first student then the second student, etc or all data for the first lab and the second lab, etc.)
b. Does it read exactly 14 labs for 40 students? Explain.
c. Add a function to print the scores so that each student's labs appear on a separate line of output. Include a statement in your main program to call this function. Your output should be labeled as follows:

```
Student 1: 80 90 70 100 60 90 85 78 93 80 70 98 89 94
Student 2: 98 85 100  99 89 90 72  0 78 98 100 65  0 56
Student 3: 85  60 25....
     .
     .
     .
```

Compile and run your program to make sure it is error free.

E. Two-dimensional Array Processing

Processing of two-dimensional arrays might include finding an average of a row or a column. Suppose in our lab scores problem, we wish to determine the lab average for the third student (remember, this means row 2). The solution to this problem consists of finding the sum of all of the entries in row 2 and dividing by the number of labs, *MAXLABS*.

```
15   sum = 0;
16   student = 2;
17   for (lab = 0; lab < MAXLABS; lab++)
18      sum += labscores[student][lab];
19   average = float(sum)/MAXLABS;
```

In general, if we wish to determine the average for the Kth student, then K-1 would replace row 2 in statement 16 above. If we wish to find an average for all 40 students, we can add an outer loop to control the student subscript as in the following code:

```
//for each student, find the lab average
for (student=0; student < MAXSTUDENTS; student++)
{
        //sum the labs for a student
        sum = 0;
        for (lab = 0; lab < MAXLABS; lab++)
                sum += labscores[student][lab];

        //find the average for the student
        average = sum/MAXLABS;

        //display the lab average
        cout << "The lab average for student #  ", student;
        cout << " was "<< average;
}
```

EXERCISE 5:   Add a function to *inlab13.cpp*, say **lab_avg**(), which finds and prints the average score made on one lab (i.e. find the average of one column of the *labscores* array). Be careful!! How many students were read from the file? Call this procedure from the main program to find the average score for each lab (and then print the answer). Compile and run your program. Turn in a listing and run of this program.

Lab 13 Files

```
//File:          inlab13.cpp
//Author:
//Purpose:       This program reads data for a computer science
//               closed lab section.

//Input:         Input for this program is from the external data
//               file inlab13.dat.  The first entry in the file
//               is the number of students in the class.  For each
//               student, their closed labs are input from the file.

//Limitations:   It is assumed that there will be no more than
//               MAXSTUDENTS students in the class and there will be
//               exactly MAXLABS labs.

//include files...
#include <iostream.h>
#include <fstream.h>

//global constants...
const int MAXSTUDENTS=40;                //maximum number of students
const int MAXLABS=14;                    //maximum number of closed labs

void main()
{
    //function prototypes...
    //function to read labs from the data file
    void read_labs(int&, int [][MAXLABS], ifstream&);

    //your function prototypes should go here!!!

    //local declarations...
    int num_students;                        //how many students are in the class
    ifstream myin ("inlab13.dat");           //input file stream
    int labscores[MAXSTUDENTS][MAXLABS];     //holds lab scores

    //read in the data for all students in the class
    read_labs(num_students, labscores, myin);

    //print the data for all students in the class
    //your function should be called here!!!!!

    //end of main...
    return;
}



//Function:      read_labs()
//Purpose:       This function reads data for students in a closed
```

```
//              lab class.  Data is read from the input file stream
//              myin.  The number of students in the lab is read
//              first.  Next, for each student, their closed labs
//              are read into the two-d array labscores.
//Assumption:   MAXLABS is a global constant which has been defined
//              previously.

void read_labs(int& num_students,        //IN:  # of students
               int labscores[][MAXLABS], //OUT: Holds the closed lab scores
               ifstream& myin)           //IN:  Input file stream
{
    //local declarations...
    int student;                         //controls which student's labs are read
    int lab;                             //controls which lab is being read

    //get the number of students in the class
    myin >> num_students;

    //outer loop controls which student
    for (student = 0; student < num_students; student++)

            //inner loop controls which lab is being read
            for (lab = 0; lab < MAXLABS; lab++)
                myin >> labscores[student][lab];

    return;
}
```

FILE: inlab13.dat

5
100 98 97 89 100 96 95 90 100 89 88 100 99 98
80 82 89 95 45 86 95 76 88 37 100 100 78 95
60 67 0 54 78 99 45 76 89 53 76 10 57 90
80 80 80 70 70 70 90 90 90 90 80 90 100 80
90 91 92 93 94 95 96 97 98 100 99 98 97 96

Lab 13 - Answer Sheet

NAME:_____

EXERCISE 1:

EXERCISE 2:

    a)

    b)

    c)

EXERCISE 3:

EXERCISE 4:

a)

b)

Lab 14

Parallel Arrays

Objectives:	To introduce the concept of parallel arrays
	To practice manipulating parallel arrays

A. Introduction to Parallel Arrays

In Lab 13 we illustrated two-dimensional arrays in our example of student lab scores. Let's briefly review that example. We had a two-dimensional table which held lab scores for a class of students. A printout of the scores in this table might appear as follows:

```
                   Lab Grades
Student
Name              1     2     3      . . .
-----------------------------------------------------------
Adams, J.        100    85    90     . . .
Brooks, B.       100    35    35     . . .
Brown, L.         50   100    90     . . .
Carson, J.        75    70    65     . . .
Dalton, F.         .     .     .     . . .
```

Notice that the majority of this table consists of the two-dimensional table of lab scores which were made by each student on the various labs. However, we might also wish to remember the names of students in addition to the scores.

This example is not uncommon. Often a collection of data contains items of different types. An array is used to store data of the same kind. Therefore an array cannot be used to store names (strings) and integer lab scores. Later we will discuss a new data structure called a record (struct in C++) which will allow an alternate solution to this problem. However, for now, we can visualize two arrays to handle the data for our budget problem. Consider the following picture.

First Array:
names

Second Array:
labsores

0	Adams, J.
1	Brooks, B.
2	Brown, L.
3	Carson, J.
	.
	.

	0	1	. . .
0	100	85	. . .
1	100	35	. . .
2	50	35	. . .
3	75	70	. . .
	.	.	. . .
	.	.	. . .

These two arrays are called **parallel arrays** because the data items with the same row subscript pertain to the same student. For example, all data for the student, Brown, L., is stored in row 2 in *names* and in row 2 in *labscores*. The declarations below could be used to declare the two parallel arrays.

```
const int NAMELENGTH  = 20;          //maximum length of a name
const int MAXSTUDENTS = 40;          //maximum number of students
const int MAXLABS     = 14;          //maximum number of labs
....

char names[MAXSTUDENTS][NAMELENGTH];     //array to hold the names
int  labscores [MAXSTUDENTS][MAXLABS];   //array to hold lab scores
....
```

EXERCISE 1:   Now let us return to the budget problem discussed in Lab 13. Suppose we wished to keep an array which described our budgeted items (rent, electric, water, etc.) as well as an array containing our budget. Show declarations for parallel arrays which could be used in this problem. In other words one row of the first array might contain the string "rent" and the same row in the second array would contain expenditures for rent for the 12 months. Assume that the maximum description for a budgeted item contains 30 characters and that the maximum number of budgeted items needed is 15.

B. Manipulating Parallel Arrays

Suppose we wished to read in data for our student's lab scores from a file *inlab14.dat* which is organized as follows:

> Line 1 contains the first student's name
> Line 2 contains the first student's scores
> Line 3 contains the second student's name
> Line 4 contains the second student's scores
> and so on....

Thus the data file might appear as:

> Adams, J.
> 100   85   90 . . .
> Brooks, B.
> 100   35   35 . . .
> Brown, L.
> 50   100   90 . . .
> . . .

Notice that to read this data, we must read in a student's name, then we must read in the student's scores. After the first student's data is read, the second student's data is read, etc.

Suppose we have written a function to read an individual student's name, say *read_name()*, and a function to enter a student's lab scores, say *read_labs()*. To read the data file, we might use the following C++ code:

```
//Function:      get_students()
//Purpose:       This function reads student names and labs from
//               a data file. This function returns the actual number of
//               students in the class.
//Assumption:    We must eliminate the carriage return after the set
//               of scores to prepare to read the next name.

void get_students       (char names[][NAMELENGTH],  //OUT:array of student names

                         int  labscores[][MAXLABS],      //OUT:array of labs
```

```
                        int&  num_students)              //OUT: the # of students
{
        //function prototypes
        void read_name(ifstream&,char[]);          //gets one name
        void read_labs(ifstream&,int []);   //gets one student's scores

        //local variables
        int i=0;                               //How many students so far?
        char CR;                               //carriage return after the scores
        ifstream myin ("inlab14.dat");         //Input file stream

        //while we aren't at the end of file and we haven't
        //exceeded our array size:
        while ((!myin.eof()) && (i < MAXSTUDENTS))
        {
                //read a student's name and place it in the ith
                //row of the names array
                read_name(myin, names[i]);

                //read a student's scores and place them into the
                //the ith row of the labs array
                read_labs(myin, labscores[i]);

                //read the carriage return after the labs to prepare
                //for the next name
                myin.get(CR);

                //Are we at the end of the file?
                myin.peek();

                //update our counter
                i++;
        }
        num_students = i;
        return;
}


//Function:       read_name()
//Purpose:        This function reads one student's name

void read_name (ifstream& myin,          //IN: the input file stream
                char student_name[])     //OUT: a student's name
{
        //local variables
        int i=0;          //counter for the character

        //get the first character
        myin.get(student_name[i]);

        //get characters for the name as long as the newline
        //character hasn't been read or we are about to exceed
```

```
//our name length. (Remember we must reserve one space
//for the null character)
while ((i < NAMELENGTH-1) && (student_name[i] != '\n'))
{
        i++;
        myin.get(student_name[i]);
}

//put the null character at the end of the string.
student_name[i]='\0';
return;
}
```

Examine the above code very carefully. It contains a new concept that we have not used before. Notice that when we called the function *read_name()*, it looks as if we sent it a single array element *names[i]* and this is precisely what we did. Remember that the two-dimensional array *names* can be thought of as a one-dimensional array of elements. Each element just happens to be a row of characters in this case. Thus the function *read_names()* reads one element (a complete name) into the ith row of the array *names*.

EXERCISE 2: Look at the call to *read_labs()*. Explain why we sent a single array element *labscores[i]* to this function when *labscores* is a two-dimensional array.

EXERCISE 3: Copy the program *inlab14.cpp* and the data file *inlab14.dat* to your account. The program contains a main function with declarations for the *names* and *labscores* arrays. It also contains the code above which reads data into the two arrays. The only piece that is missing to allow the data file to be read is the *read_labs()* function. Type in the following heading for the *read_labs()* function and insert the code for this function into the program. The function should read exactly MAXLABS lab scores for a student.

```
void read_labs    (ifstream& myin,           //IN: input file stream
                   int set_of_labs[])         //OUT:lab scores for one student
```

EXERCISE 4: Add code to **inlab14.cpp** to print the two arrays in the following form:

Student	Labs			
=======	====	===	===	....
Adams, J.	100	85	90	....
Brooks, B.	100	35	35	....
Brown, L.	50	100	90	....
.	.	.	.	....

Remember that the names are strings (we made them strings by adding the null character).

To print a string, all we have to do is use a *cout* statement to print the entire string.

EXERCISE 5: Also included in the code is a function called student_avg() which calculates the lab average for one student. Add code to the program which uses this function and produces the output below. Turn in a listing, compile and run of the modified *inlab14.cpp*.

Student	Lab average
Adams, J.	92.50
Brooks, B.	53.96
Brown, L.	85.72
.	.
.	.
.	.

Lab 14 Files

```
//File:          inlab14.cpp
//Author:
//Purpose:       This program reads data for students in a
//               computer science lab class from a file "inlab14.dat".
//               Data for each student includes the student's name and
//               scores on a set of labs.

//include files...
#include <iostream.h>
#include <fstream.h>

//global constants...
const int NAMELENGTH=20;        //maximum length of a name
const int MAXLABS=14;           //maximum number of labs
const int MAXSTUDENTS=40;       //maximum number of students

void main()
{
    //function prototypes...

    //function to read data for all students
    void get_students (char [][NAMELENGTH],
                   int [][MAXLABS],int&);

    //local variables...
    int howmany;                                  //how many students
    char names[MAXSTUDENTS][NAMELENGTH];          //student names
    int labscores [MAXSTUDENTS][MAXLABS];         //student labs

    //get the data for all students
    get_students(names, labscores, howmany);

    //print the names and labs here!!!!

    return;
}



//Function:      get_students()
//Purpose:       This function reads student names and labs from
//               a data file. This function returns the actual
//               number of students in the class.
//Assumption:    We must eliminate the carriage return after the set
//               of scores to prepare to read the next name.

void get_students (char names[][NAMELENGTH],     //OUT:array of student names
               int  labscores[][MAXLABS],        //OUT:array of labs
               int& num_students)                //OUT:# of students
```

```
{
    //function prototypes...
    void read_name(ifstream&,char[]);              //read a name
    void read_labs(ifstream&,int []);              //read student's scores

    //local variables
    int i=0;                                       //How many students so far?
    char CR;                                       //carriage return after the scores
    ifstream myin ("inlab14.dat");                 //Input file stream

    //while we aren't at the end of file and we haven't
    //exceeded our array size:
    while ((!myin.eof()) && (i < MAXSTUDENTS))
    {
        //read a student's name and place it in the ith
        //row of the names array
        read_name(myin, names[i]);

        //read a student's scores and place them into the
        //the ith row of the labs array
        read_labs(myin, labscores[i]);

        //read the carriage return after the labs to prepare
        //for the next name
        myin.get(CR);

        //Are we at the end of the file?
        myin.peek();

        //update our counter
        i++;
    }
    num_students = i;
    return;
}


//Function:      read_name()
//Purpose:       This function reads one student's name

void read_name (ifstream& myin,                    //IN: the input file stream
                char student_name[])               //OUT: a student's name
{
    //local variables
    int i=0;                                       //counter for the character

    //get the first character
    myin.get(student_name[i]);

    //get characters for the name as long as the newline
    //character hasn't been read or we are about to exceed
    //our name length. (Remember we must reserve one space
```

```
    //for the null character)
    while ((i < NAMELENGTH-1) && (student_name[i] != '\n'))
    {
        i++;
        myin.get(student_name[i]);
    }

    //put the null character at the end of the string.
    student_name[i]='\0';
    return;
}



//Function:      read_labs()
//Purpose:       Your read_labs() function should go here!!!!!



//Function:      student_avg()
//Purpose:       This function receives lab scores made by one
//               student and calculates the student's lab
//               average.  The average is returned to the
//               calling program.

float student_avg (int student_labs[])      //IN:  a student's lab scores
{
        //local declarations...
        int labsum = 0;                     //the sum of the labs

        //calculate the sum of the labs
        for (int i = 0; i < MAXLABS; i++)
            labsum = labsum + student_labs[i];

        //return the average
        return float (labsum)/MAXLABS;
}
```

FILE: inlab14.dat

Mouse, Mick E.
100 90 75 80 90 45 67 89 100 56 78 100 89 56
Mouse, Minn E.
95 96 97 98 100 100 90 90 91 92 93 94 95 96
Hood, Rob N.
90 90 90 90 90 90 90 90 90 90 90 90 90 90
Rella, Cindy
60 70 80 90 100 95 96 97 98 100 92 91 90 100
Duck, Don L.
80 81 82 83 84 85 86 87 88 89 90 91 92 93
Einstein, Al
100 100 100 100 100 100 100 100 100 100 100 100 100 100

Lab 14 - Answer Sheet

NAME:_____

EXERCISE 1:

EXERCISE 2: